UGARIT AND MINOAN CRETE

UGARIT AND MINOAN CRETE

THE BEARING OF THEIR TEXTS

ON THE ORIGINS OF WESTERN CULTURE

by CYRUS H. GORDON

W · W · NORTON & COMPANY · INC ·
New York

CONTENTS

FOREWORD

While Ugaritic literature is of antiquarian interest in its own right, its significance derives mainly from the light it throws on the origin and nature of early Greek and Hebrew literatures. Ugaritic has already put Old Testament studies on a new footing. Its impact on early Greek literature is still unfolding. Books have been written on Ugarit and ancient Israel,[1] and on how Ugarit links Homer and the Bible.[2] But something new, of a crucial nature, is now to be added: the growing evidence of the Minoan inscriptions showing that until sometime after 1500 B.C., Greece, Ugarit, and Israel all belonged to the same cultural sphere, in which the most important linguistic and cultural element, in the varying and composite makeup of all three, was Phoenician. This development will inevitably exert a profound effect on our concept of ancient history, Hellenic origins, and the Hebrew Bible—in short, the roots and character of our own Western civilization. For this reason, Ugaritic literature takes on a fresh meaning and is broadening our horizons.

The contents of this book rest on the original sources. Naturally it cannot repeat all of the evidence that is well established and available in other publications. But I have documented, from the primary ancient sources, every point that marks a departure from common knowledge.

Our subject is in a dynamic stage with wide and varied implications. The latter are sometimes expressed in footnotes, which are therefore often as important as—and occasionally more important than—the accompanying text.

[1] E.g., A. S. Kapelrud, *The Ras Shamra Discoveries and the Old Testament*, Norman, Okla., 1963; C. F. Pfeiffer, *Ras Shamra and the Bible*, Grand Rapids, 1962.

[2] C. H. Gordon, "Homer and the Bible," *Hebrew Union College Annual*, 26, 1955, pp. 43–108, and *The Common Background of Greek and Hebrew Civilizations*, New York, 1965; H. Haag, *Homer, Ugarit und das Alte Testament* (*Biblische Beiträge* NF 2), 1962.

I hope that the reader will share with me not only the facts but also the adventure of discovering them and following them to their logical conclusions.

Cyrus H. Gordon
Brookline, Mass.
June 21, 1965

UGARIT AND MINOAN CRETE

Chapter I

UGARIT AND ITS SIGNIFICANCE

In 1928 a peasant accidentally plowed into an ancient tomb near the coast of northern Syria. The French authorities were notified and lost no time in sponsoring an archaeological expedition there. One of the two codirectors of the first campaign was Claude Schaeffer, who sensed the importance of the site from the start. The tomb discovered by the peasant was Mycenaean in style, though found on Semitic soil. The nearby mound of Ras Shamra, to which it was related, therefore appeared to be a probable link between Canaan and the Aegean in Mycenaean times (*ca.* 1500–1200 B.C.). The first campaign yielded cuneiform tablets in a new script early in 1929. Fortunately, they were turned over to Professor Charles Virolleaud, the eminent Assyriologist, for study and publication. It is to the lasting credit of French scholarship that the tablets were published in record time before the close of 1929. As a result three scholars,[1] independently and almost simultaneously, succeeded in deciphering enough of the new script and language in 1930 to guarantee complete decipherment within a few years.

Except for the interruption imposed by the Second World War, Professor Schaeffer has gone back to dig at Ras Shamra year after year, each time finding a rich harvest of texts and monuments, although more than a third of a century has passed since the epoch-

[1] The first to publish his results was Hans Bauer; the second, Edouard Dhorme; the third, Charles Virolleaud. See C. H. Gordon, *UT* (*Ugaritic Textbook*), Rome, 1965, p. 1 (§ 1.3).

making campaign of 1929.

Ras Shamra ("Fennel Head") is the native Arabic name for the
mound that marks the site of ancient Ugarit. The city was the
capital of the small Ugaritic Kingdom, and was situated fairly close
to the shore. Its port was located at the nearby Minet al-Bayda,
"White Harbor," as the natives now call it in Arabic.

Ugarit derived its importance from its location. In its heyday,
from about 1400 to 1200 B.C., the center of what was destined to
become the cradle of Western civilization was the East Mediterranean. To the east lay Mesopotamia, the outstanding pioneer in
literate culture and international trade. To the south was situated
Egypt, the aristocrat of the international Order, whose ships sailed
the Sea and whose victorious armies had reached the Euphrates in
the mid-fifteenth century B.C. under the leadership of Thutmose III.
To the north was the empire of the Hittites, that became the leading power in Asia after defeating the Mitannians in north Mesopotamia.[2] To the west were the Sea People, among whom the
Mycenaean Greeks were emerging as the dominant factor.[3] Ugarit
itself was located near the northwest corner of what we may call
Canaan, the land that nurtured a number of linguistically related
groups, including the Phoenicians and Hebrews. Thus Ugarit was
the heir of the great cultures that had gone before, from Sumer to
Egypt. Ugarit had the closest relations with people such as the
Hittites and Hurrians, who were of prime importance in Mycenaean
times, but were destined to disappear and require the spade of the
archaeologist to revive their memory. Ugarit was intimately connected with the Phoenicians, who were spreading East Mediterranean civilization wherever possible by sea. Most important of all
—though the ancients could hardly have realized it—Ugarit was
in contact with the forerunners of the classical Greeks and Hebrews,
who were destined to found Western civilization by their combined

[2] It was the Hittite King Shuppiluliuma I (*ca.* 1380–1346 B.C.) who defeated the Mitannian King Tushratta (whose reign ended around 1354 B.C.).

[3] A milestone in the ascendance of the Mycenaean Greeks was their conquest of Knossos, which the adherents of Arthur Evans date sometime during
the second half of the fifteenth century B.C., but which the followers of L. R.
Palmer put around 1200 B.C.

and parallel achievements.

We need not and must not withhold credit from the Ugaritians themselves. They were a talented and enterprising people in their own right. But they were lucky to be living in the right place at the right time: at the crossroads of the Western world when the seeds of Hellas and Israel had been planted and were producing their first fruits.

The archaeological finds at Ugarit are rich and varied.[4] They range from palace and temple architecture to potsherds. They include handsome jewelry and royal seals. The finds at Ugarit are interrelated with the art and monuments of the whole Amarna Order, embracing Babylonia, Anatolia, Egypt, and the Aegean.

Artifacts are relegated to secondary importance in historical studies whenever a civilization is literate. We rely heavily on artifacts for investigating Neolithic cultures, before the dawn of writing, because there are no texts from which we can derive more precise historic data. The reason prehistoric Tell Halaf pottery is so much more important than historic Egyptian or Sumerian pottery is that the Tell Halaf culture is preliterate, whereas Egypt and Sumer have left us so many inscriptions that we do not depend primarily on the ceramics for reconstructing the history of those countries in literate times.

One of the hardest things for a seasoned specialist to do is to make the adjustment required by the first discovery of texts in his field. At the moment when authoritative and generally accepted speculation must yield to the plain meaning of newly discovered or newly deciphered texts, many a specialist is found wanting in the flexibility needed to unlearn the false and to comprehend the true. There are veteran Minoan scholars who have not really come to grips with the fact that with the decipherment of Linear A, their field has emerged from prehistory into history

A tacit assumption has it that Israel and Greece were independent cultures, poles apart. Speciously, a case can be made for such a

---

[4] The preliminary reports appear in the French journal *Syria*. The final publications appear in two series of volumes by Schaeffer and his associates: *Ugaritica* (devoted mainly to archaeological materials) and *PRU* (*Palais royal d'Ugarit*), Paris (devoted mainly to texts).

view. For when did Israel produce a Parthenon, and when did
Greece bring forth an Isaiah? But the Ugaritic epics, as will appear
below, have unmistakable and organic parallels that link the pre-
prophetic Hebrews with the prephilosophical Greeks.[5] If one follows the testimony of the texts, it will become evident that the
monuments, correctly understood, confirm that testimony.

Archaeologists have rightly been pointing out genuine relation-
ships between the architecture of Asiatic sites in Canaan and Anatolia and the Minoan palaces of Crete.[6] This has disturbed some
writers who want to keep Minoan civilization free of Asiatic—and
particularly Semitic—"contamination." They point to the distinctive
art of the Minoans. They say (and rightly so) that a palace city on
Minoan Crete is not the same as Mari, Alalakh, Ugarit, and other
Asiatic sites[7] (whose excavators have pointed out Minoan ana-
logues with equal cogency!). What is often misunderstood is that
relationship and individuality are not mutually exclusive. It would
be hard to imagine two cultures more different than those of Athens
and Sparta in the Age of Pericles, and yet because they were both
Greek we know that they were related. How do we know that an
English village with thatched roofs belongs to the same cultural
sphere as Manhattan with its skyscrapers? Certainly not from the
architecture, but because we happen to know that both are parts
of the English-speaking segment of Western civilization. The news-
papers in the homes of the English village and in the apartments of
Manhattan are better historical and cultural criteria than the buildings.

The quality and abundance of the Ugaritic texts have put the
monuments of Ugarit somewhat in the shade. The inscriptions in-

[5] The general scheme of things is as follows: (a) in the second millennium
B.C. Greeks and Hebrews were members of the same international order in
the East Mediterranean; (b) then in the first millennium B.C., down to the
fourth century, the Greeks and Hebrews each produced their distinctive classical contributions; (c) but with Alexander's Conquest in the fourth century
B.C., both people were thrown together again in the Hellenistic Order.

[6] For a comprehensive study of Minoan civilization, see R. W. Hutchinson,
Prehistoric Crete, Baltimore, 1962.

[7] Note J. W. Graham, *Palaces of Crete*, Princeton, 1962; and "Minoan
Palaces and Near Eastern Palaces," in *Mycenaean Studies, Wingspread, 1961*
(edited by E. L. Bennett), Madison, Wis., 1964, pp. 195–215.

clude a variety of scripts: Sumero-Akkadian syllabic cuneiform, the native alphabetic cuneiform, Egyptian hieroglyphs, Hittite hieroglyphs, and the Aegean syllabary. An even larger variety of languages is represented: Sumerian, Akkadian, Hurrian, Hittite, Egyptian, Ugaritic, and whatever language(s) turn out to be expressed in the Aegean syllabary. Ugaritic, Hurrian, and probably Akkadian were written in both syllabic and alphabetic cuneiform at Ugarit.

The Ugaritic texts are particularly important for the native poetic literature, which may be divided into epics about people and myths about the gods. But there are many other types of texts in Ugaritic, including administrative records, royal epistles, and school texts. Even the simplest school texts are of extraordinary interest; they consist of the letters of the alphabet already listed in the fixed traditional order: *a b g ḫ d h w z ḥ ṭ y k š l m d n ẓ s ʿ p ṣ q r ṯ ǵ t i u ś.* This embodies the same alphabetic tradition that has come down to us through the Phoenicians/Hebrews, Greeks, and Romans. To be sure, changes have occurred during the long chain of transmission, but *a b – d – – – h – – k l m n – p q r – t*[8] in our English ABC appear in the same sequence as in the Ugaritic alphabet, not by accident, but for clear historic reasons. The Hebrew sequence of *a b g d h w z ḥ ṭ y k l m n s ʿ p ṣ q r – t* agrees even more strikingly with the Ugaritic for the simple reason that they were used for closely related Semitic languages in the vicinity of Phoenicia.[9] This alphabet is the most important and useful single invention of civilized man. Greece and Israel shared it—and much else besides.[10]

---

[8] Actually, other letters in the English ABC are still in their old Ugaritic positions, but technical explanations would be required to account for their apparent modification.

[9] Cuneiform, including Ugaritic, is nearly always written from left to right. A few of the Ugaritic texts are written from right to left (like Hebrew), with fewer signs than the regular Ugaritic script with thirty letters. It is quite likely that this right-to-left alphabet has only twenty-two letters, like Hebrew. The fact that two of these right-to-left texts have been found in Palestine (one at Beth-Shemesh and the other on Mount Tabor) suggests that it was a medium of native literacy from North Syria to Palestine in proto-Hebrew times. See *UT*, p. 16 (§ 3.6).

[10] Notably the literature that it recorded, as is spelled out in Gordon, *The Common Background of Greek and Hebrew Civilizations.*

Another type of school text is the polyglot vocabulary. Any international culture requires the services of translators. The scribes of Ugarit were called on to handle a number of languages. Some of the vocabularies list words in three parallel columns: Sumerian, Akkadian, and Hurrian. Two of the vocabulary tablets list each word in four columns, adding Ugaritic to the above three languages. Obviously a community that fostered a school system in which the advanced scribes studied texts to qualify them in four languages at a time, was highly sophisticated.[11] Akkadian was commonly used for legal contracts and international affairs.[12] These are our main source for our knowledge of the royal, aristocratic, and administrative circles, as well as for the history of Ugarit [13] and its dealings with other nations.

Hurrian texts, more often than not, deal with religion, ritual, and magic. Next to the Northwest Semites, who constituted the majority of the Ugaritic population, the largest single component of the people was Hurrian. Hurrians throughout the second millennium were spread all over the Near East, from Babylonia to Egypt, and from Canaan to Anatolia and the Aegean.

The proper names in the various categories of tablets from Ugarit are of great importance in determining the ethnography of the population and the origins of the religious, military, social, and other institutions. A study of the names tells us the ethnic composition of the community much as a telephone book can today. In addition to the legion Northwest Semitic and the many Hurrian names, the Ugaritic onomasticon has Egyptian, Mesopotamian, East Mediterranean, Hittite, and other Anatolian names.[14]

[11] As this statement implies, the earliest Greek and Hebrew literatures stem from a highly cultured and international milieu. There is nothing primitive about either of them. Neither the Greeks nor the Hebrews were pioneers in literacy. They were both preceded by Minoan literacy (which began around 1800 B.C.), which in turn was preceded by Sumero-Akkadian and Egyptian literacy (from shortly after 3000 B.C.). So far, the earliest people whom we can call literate are the Sumerians; next come the Egyptians.

[12] Nearly all the Akkadian tablets are being published by Jean Nougayrol in *PRU.* See *PRU* III, 1955, for the legal contracts, and *PRU* IV, 1956, for the international archives.

[13] See also Mario Liverani, *Storia di Ugarit (nell'età' degli archivi politici),* 1962, for a sketch of the political history of Ugarit.

[14] *Cf.* Roy Uyechi, *A Study of Ugaritic Alphabetic Personal Names,* an unpublished doctoral dissertation, Brandeis University, Waltham, Mass., 1961.

The Ugaritic texts (roughly 1400–1200 B.C.) fall within the My-cenaean Age, to use Aegean terminology; [15] or the Amarna [16] and Ramesside [17] ages, if we are to employ the nomenclature of Near Eastern studies. The Amarna Age (late fifteenth and early four-teenth centuries B.C.) saw the entire Near East form an Order centered on the East Mediterranean. The period derives its name from the collection of clay tablets found between 1887 and 1933 at Tell el-Amarna, the capital of Ikhnaton in Egypt. Most of the tablets are Babylonian letters exchanged between the Pharaohs [18] and the monarchs of Mesopotamia, Anatolia, Canaan (including Ugarit), and Cyprus. The Order consisted of nations in diplomatic and commercial contact with each other. Egypt was the aristocrat of the international Order. At the beginning of the Age, Mitanni was the leading Asiatic power; at the end, the Hittites occupied that role. The significance of the Amarna Age is that in it the old cultures of Mesopotamia and Egypt met in the East Mediterranean, to intermingle with the Northwest Semites, Hurrians, Indo-Europeans, and other stocks represented in the area. No mainland city was more at the center of things than Ugarit. The ancestors of the classical Hebrews and Greeks were then on the scene in the Levant. The Ugaritic texts therefore give us the backdrop to the earliest Greek and Hebrew literatures.

[15] The best literary texts were copied in the form we now have them dur-ing the reign of Niqmad II, who ruled Ugarit down to about 1345 B.C.

[16] The two Amarna Age Pharaohs were Amenophis III (*ca.* 1413–1377 B.C.) and Amenophis IV, better known as Ikhnaton (*ca.* 1377–1358 B.C.). Cf. W. A. Ward, *The Spirit of Ancient Egypt*, Beirut, 1965, pp. 69–75, 165–166.

[17] The reign of Ramses II (*ca.* 1301–1234 B.C.) marked the height of the Ramesside Age.

[18] The most convenient and extensive edition is S. A. B. Mercer, *The Tell el-Amarna Tablets*, Vols. I and II, Toronto, 1939. The older edition by J. A. Knudtzon (*Die El-Amarna-Tafeln, Vorderasiatische Bibliothek*, Leipzig, 1907–15) is, however, more reliable.

Chapter II

UGARITIC LITERATURE AND ITS GRECO-HEBREW AFFINITIES

The East Mediterranean was, as we have noted, the scene of an international synthesis in the centuries when Ugarit flourished. Not only isolated cultural details, but whole cultural complexes were then being transmitted over wide areas. This process was due largely to the mobility of guildsmen, whose technical services were in demand over wide areas, transcending national, linguistic, and ethnic boundaries. While buildings were not transferred from land to land, builders were. This explains much of the spread of certain architectural features. There was no point in importing fragile ceramics for ordinary household use. It was the potters, rather than their wares, who could move without breakage.[1] Warriors, organized into guilds according to their functions, were so mobile that the same guilds were usually represented in both opposing armies. When Egypt battled against her Asiatic foes, members of the *maryannu* guild of charioteers could be found on both sides.[2]

Traders and even priests ranked among the mobile guildsmen and as such wandered far and wide. Thus Ugaritic text 81[3] mentions traders (*mkrm* = Hebrew *môkᵉrîm*) and two guilds of priests:

---

[1] This does not mean that goods were not imported. They were—including fragile pottery. Yet at the same time we must realize that craftsmen were imported too (II Kings 24:14; *Odyssey* 17:382–386).

[2] War, of course, sets in motion waves of refugees who are even better carriers of culture than the troops who have caused their plight.

[3] The alphabetic Ugaritic texts are available in *UT*.

khnm (= Hebrew *kôhᵃnîm*) and *qdšm* (= Hebrew *qᵉdēshîm*).
Though the *qᵉdēshîm* were eliminated from the cult of Judah by
King Josiah around 621 B.C. (II Kings 23:7), the legitimate priests
of the Jews have continued to be called *kôhᵃnîm* throughout biblical
history, and down to the present.[4]

The international spread of religious guilds helped disseminate
cultic practices and religious beliefs far and wide. Since Ugarit and
Israel were both in Canaan, the cultic connections between them
are close. Thus the term inaccurately translated in the English
Bible as "peace offering" is identical in Hebrew (*shᵉlāmîm*) and
Ugaritic (spelled *šlmm* consonantally). El is the head of the pantheon in Israel as well as in Ugarit. And although biblical monotheism eventually eliminated the worship of the Ugaritic-Canaanite
gods, including Baal, Anath, Asherah, Astarte, Yamm, Dagon,
Shaḥar, Shemesh, Yārēᵃḥ,[5] the Hebrews were not only exposed to
them through their pagan neighbors, but as the Prophets tell us, frequently committed apostasy by worshiping them down to the time
of the Babylonian Exile in the sixth century B.C.

The actual names of the West Semitic gods do not usually survive
in Greek; "Adon-is" (from *Ādôn*, "lord," an epithet of Baal at
Ugarit) is an exception. But that other West Semitic names of gods
had reached Greek soil is quite clear from other evidence. Pausanius
(2:25:10) records that a site near Epidauris used to be called
"Sapyselaton," which is distinctively Ugaritic.[6] "Sapys" corresponds
to Ugaritic *špš*, the sun "goddess" (*elat*). The form of "Sapys"
(with *p*, instead of the *m* that normally appears in Semitic *Shamash*) and its feminine gender (in contrast to Akkadian *Shamash*,
which is masculine) link "Sapyselaton" unmistakably with the
Ugaritic branch of Northwest Semitic.

---

[4] This illustrates the fact the Hebrews sometimes borrowed from (as in
the case of the *kôhᵃnîm*), and at other times reacted against (as in the case
of the *qᵉdēshîm*), their Canaanite milieu.

[5] A pithy description of each god is given by M. H. Pope and W. Röllig
in their monograph "Syrien: Die Mythologie der Ugariter und Phönizer,"
appearing in *Wörterbuch der Mythologie* (edited by H. W. Haussig), Stuttgart,
1962, pp. 219–312 and plates I–VIII.

[6] M. C. Astour makes this observation in his important book *Hellenosemitica*
Leiden, 1965, p. 103, n. 1.

The widespread feature of "the mountain of the gods" is frequently mentioned in Ugaritic literature. The sacred mountain was
called "Saphon," which is also attested in the Bible, where it is
sometimes identified with Jerusalem.[7] In any given culture that is
spread far in time or place, the location of the sacred mountain is
likely to shift. There is many a Mount Olympos in the Greek world.
Moreover, the holy mountain can be transferred to a different locale
with a different name. Thus Mount Ida (whether of Crete or the
Troad) parallels Olympos when conditions demand. "Saphon" des-
ignated several different sacred mountains, depending on when
and where the devotees lived. Moreover, the sacred mountain of
Israel shifted to Mount Sinai, Mount Ebal or Mount Gerizim,
Mount Zion, and so on, depending on the period and location of
Yahweh's followers. In Ugaritic literature, Baal dwells on the
heights of Saphon. (El, however, resides at the source of the two
cosmic rivers.)

El, the head of the pantheon, is also called Thôr, "the Bull." El
is identified with the God of Israel, and it is interesting that in
Judges 6:25 he is mentioned as *hash-Shôr*, "the Bull." Inasmuch as
this word for "bull" occurs in all the ancient Semitic languages with
the regular sound shifts proper to original Semitic words, it cannot
easily be regarded as a borrowing from elsewhere. In Arabic it is
thawr-, in Hebrew and Akkadian it is *shôr-*, in Aramaic it is *tôr-;*
it cannot be separated from Greek and Latin *taur-.* The simplest
explanation is that it entered the Aegean through Semitic channels,
and fanned out in the Indo-European world with the spread of the
Minoans and their cultural heirs. Verbal similarity is not the only
basis for this view. The role of the bull in religion and sport [8] is
strikingly similar in both the Semitic and Indo-European segments
of Mediterranean civilization, especially in the Minoan-Mycenaean
sphere.

El is the principal figure in a religious drama (text 52) telling
how the Great God sired progeny from two human wives. First they

---

[7] E.g., Psalm 48:3 (48:2 in the King James Bible). In Isaiah 14:13, however, Saphon is some distant and inaccessible Olympos.

[8] See *The Common Background of Greek and Hebrew Civilizations*, pp.
51–52, 70, 275–276.

bore him Dawn and Dusk; later they bore him the Seven Good Gods of fertility, who symbolize a seven-year cycle of plenty. This text is important for many reasons. It is a milestone in the evolution of the drama, for it is equipped with stage directions and is definitely a production of myth and ritual in dramatic form. It also shows that the sabbatical cycle of the Old Testament is a religious and agricultural institution taken over by the Hebrews from the older, native population of Canaan. It anticipates the biblical books of Hosea and Ezekiel (23:1 ff.) in attributing fertility [9] to the conjugal relationship of God [10] or his prophet [11] with two women. The biblical prophets could hardly have intended this theme to be taken literally. The Ugaritic text rather suggests that Hosea and Ezekiel were drawing on an old literary theme for poetic imagery much as we draw on Greco-Roman mythology today.

In other Ugaritic texts concerning El, Asherah appears as his consort who bore him "the seventy" gods. In popular religion, Asherah persisted as El's consort in Judah until the purifying effect of the Exile. The account of Josiah's reform suggests that the women dedicated to the cult of Asherah in the Jerusalem Temple (II Kings 23:7) [12] were considered to be in the service of Yahweh's wife. Needless to say, Josiah put a stop to it.

It often happens in the history of pantheons that younger gods eclipse the older ones as objects of adoration. As Zeus eclipses his father Cronus and grandfather Uranus, Baal and Anath are young gods who outshine the older El and Asherah in the mythological texts. Baal and Anath are the main deities (in role, though not in rank) in the bulk of the myths.

Several themes are woven into the Baal and Anath Cycle. The wars of Baal and Anath are prominent. Anath nearly annihilates mankind before she is sated with slaughter and spares the survivors. On another occasion she boasts of aiding Baal against many a foe,

[9] Quite clearly in Hosea (4:3; 6:3; 9:16; and others); by implication in Ezekiel.

[10] So in Ezekiel 23.

[11] The Prophet Hosea marries the women, but they stand for Israel and Judah, who figure as the wives, so to speak, of God.

[12] However garbled this may be in the Bible translations, this is crystal-clear in the original Hebrew.

including the monster of evil, Leviathan. The slaying of the seven-headed Leviathan by the god(s) of goodness, shows that the dualistic conflict between good and evil entered the biblical tradition with the absorption of the pre-Hebraic heritage of Canaan. Psalm 74:14 attributes the victory over the many-headed Leviathan to Yahweh. The terminology (not only "Leviathan," but also his epithets, such as "the evil serpent," "the crooked serpent," and "Tannin," as in Isaiah 27:1) leaves no doubt, for it is verbally identical in Ugaritic and Hebrew. We are dealing with a specific borrowing, not with the reappearance of a universal theme.

Baal's kingship has to be won and defended by battle. With the help of two magic clubs given to him by the god of craftsmanship (Kothar-and-Ḥasis), Ball vanquishes the sea god Yamm ("Sea") and wrests the kingship from him. Baal also has to contend periodically with Mot, the god of death and sterility. Since the periodicity of the struggles between Baal and Mot is given as seven years, the struggles must be associated with the sabbatical cycle,[13] whereby years of plenty, or of famine, were grouped in sevens in the minds of the people.

After Baal achieves kingship, he needs a palace. The palace is to be of huge dimensions, built of gold, silver, and lapis lazuli, and supported by columns made from the cedars of Lebanon. The architect is none other than Kothar-and-Ḥasis, who proposes that a window be included. Baal for a while resists, but at last agrees to this recommendation.[14] But through the window comes misfortune, probably in the person of Mot, whose lethal housebreaking through a window reverberates in Jeremiah (9:20; 9:21 in the King James Bible). The mythological erection of Baal's palace is to be compared

---

[13] The annual death and resurrection of Baal (and for that matter also of Tammuz and Osiris) must not be read from Frazer's *Golden Bough* into the ancient texts. I demonstrated that we are dealing not with annual but with sabbatical cyclicity, back in 1949 (*Ugaritic Literature*, Rome, 1949, pp. 3–5), and this view has gradually been gaining acceptance; note Pope and Röllig, pp. 263–264.

[14] The excavated buildings at Ugarit suggest that windows were not part of the old local tradition. Baal therefore wanted no windows in his palace. The architecture of Crete, however, called for windows, which is why Kothar-and-Ḥasis, whose atelier was on Caphtor (Crete), insisted on them. Thus Ugaritic literature reflects the introduction of windowed palaces from Crete.

with the historic building of Solomon's Temple. In both cases, the edifice was required because the god had grown in stature and needed an impressive home. In both cases we are dealing with Phoenician craftsmanship, imported from the artistic center of the Phoenician world. The cedars of Lebanon in both cases were used as material. Solomon got Hiram of Tyre to provide the best Phoenician materials and workmanship. The Ugaritic texts, however, hark back to conditions around the middle of the second millennium, when Phoenician civilization was centered on Minoan Crete. Kothar-and-Ḥasis is represented as coming to Baal from Caphtor (Crete); his name is pure Semitic. All this can only mean that Crete was part of the same Northwest Semitic sphere as Ugarit, culturally, religiously, and linguistically. As Solomon (in the tenth century B.C.) turned to Phoenicia, so Ugarit (around the middle of the second millennium B.C.) looked to Crete, for the best art in the contemporary West Semitic sphere.

Baal and Mot, being opposites, are natural enemies. On one occasion when Baal is summoned to face Mot in the underworld, Baal mates with a heifer, who in time bears him a bull calf as a son.[15]

---

[15] We should distinguish between the cult of the old bull (identified with El) and the cult of the young bull calf. The calf born to Baal is called *mt* (pronounced something like *moshe*), a name of Egyptian derivation; *cf.* the many -*mose* names, such as Thut-mose, "Thoth is born." Moses ("Mose-s," *Moshe* in Hebrew) is apparently named after the calf born to the Canaanite Baal, because true Egyptians never used *Mose* without another element, such as *Thut-* (Thutmose), *Raʿ-* (Ramose), *Aḥ-* (Ahmose), and the like. That the family of Moses was devoted to the cult of the calf is supported by the fact that it was his brother Aaron who presided over the setting up of the Golden Calf while Moses was getting the Law on Sinai. I Kings 12:28–29 tells of the Golden Calves worshiped by Israel in the shrines at Bethel and Dan, where they were regarded as the gods who had brought Israel out of Egypt. It is interesting to note that the consonantal text of Judges 18:30 attributes the cult at Dan to Jonathan, son of Gershom, son of Moses. A raised letter has been inserted scribally to alter "Moses" into "Manasseh," so as to whitewash the descendants of Moses. But the text is clear, and scholars are generally agreed that Jonathan is the grandson of the Lawgiver Moses. The agony of Moses is apparent once we realize that he had not only to elevate a nation from idolatry to monotheism, but also to contend with the opposition of his own family. His failure with his own descendants is all too apparent. The historic triumph of the Lawgiver is darkened by the personal tragedy of a great man who shapes the future of mankind but cannot impart his message to his own family. There is a good reason why the descendants of Moses have no place in the mainstream of Judaism.

Copulation between man and beast thus found a place in Canaanite religion. In all probability, this rite was acted out by a
priest and a heifer in the course of a cultic drama, because the
whole religion hinged on the fertility cult reflected in the mythological texts. The sharp Hebrew reaction to this bestiality is expressed
in Scripture, which clearly states that such abominations had de-
filed the inhabitants of Canaan (Leviticus 18:23–24). Much of
Hebrew religion and morality is the Israelite reaction to Canaanite
practices.

While we do not have abundant textual material bearing on
Dagon, we may conclude that he was quite important, since his
temple has been unearthed at Ugarit, and sometimes Baal is called
Dagon's Son. In the Old Testament, Dagon is the chief god of the
Philistines. The name "Dag-on" seems to be formed from *dāg*,
"fish," plus the suffix *-ôn*, an appropriate name for the god of a sea
people such as the Philistines, who came from Crete. The occurrence of the name spelled syllabically *Da-gu-na* in the Minoan
tablets from Hagia Triada is not surprising.

One of the Ugaritic texts (no. 77) belongs to the moon cult, and
describes the wedding between the Canaanite moon god Yariḫ and
the Sumero-Akkadian moon goddess Nikkal. The tablet is of interest
because it reflects the human institution of marriage and contains
a description of the ceremony, with references to bride-price, dowry,
and other payments. The purpose of the mythological wedding is
fertility in keeping with the lunar agricultural calendar. It is pre-
dicted, through an annunciation formula anticipating the Bible,
that the union will be fertile and produce offspring. The text states
that "the virgin will give birth" and "lo the maid will bear a son"—
a formula that reverberates in the famous Immanuel prophecy in
Isaiah 7:14.

The occurrence in a Ugaritic text of *Yw-il* as El's son has stirred
up some understandable controversy. But the text is clear and the
reading makes sense. The form *Yaw-* or *Yô* occurs early for "Yahweh." [16] With *-il* added, it is exactly the Hebrew name *Yô-ēl*, "Joel."

---

[16] It is embedded in the name of Moses' mother, "Jochebed" (written *Yw-kbd*
in Hebrew), and must therefore be pre-Mosaic in Israel.

That development, whereby a son-god becomes the great God, should not surprise anyone acquainted with the history of religion. Israel's monotheism is the more remarkable because of its pagan antecedents. By identifying a particular god (Yaw- or Yahweh) with the head of the pantheon (El), and equating him with the principle of godhood (Elohim), the Hebrews arrived at the monotheism that has taken root in Western civilization.

Two major poems from Ugarit may be called epics rather than myths because they deal with human characters, albeit in contact with the gods who affect their destiny. In this respect the Ugaritic epics of Aqhat and of Kret resemble Homeric epic and the Patriarchal Narratives of Genesis, whose heroes and heroines are often confronted by gods.

The *Epic of Aqhat* was known to the Hebrews. Levi's son Qehat ("Kohath" in the English Bible) bears a variant of the same name, and Ezekiel (14:14; 28:3) mentions by name Danel (Aqhat's father —"Danel" is a shorter form of "Daniel"), a virtuous and wise hero of old who survived catastrophe with his progeny. This is of interest not only per se, but also because it illustrates the fact that Ugaritic literature provides us with some of the pre-Hebrew classics of Canaan on which the Bible authors drew, as we today draw on the Hebrew, Greek and Roman classics.

The tale of Danel and Aqhat starts with the scene in which Danel, whose only child is a daughter, beseeches the gods to bless him with a model son. To accomplish this he performs the proper rites, which include incubation and offering the right sacrifices to propitiate the gods. His destined wife (Danatay) must bear the son. To sire the son from another woman is out of the question. This closely parallels the birth of Isaac. Abraham must beget him from Sarah, and not from any other woman. To achieve his goal, Abraham undergoes incubation (Genesis 15:12) and also performs the proper sacrifices to secure the impregnation of Sarah with the long-sought model son.

After fulfilling the rites and sacrifices, Danel impregnates his wife successfully with the model son, who is to be named Aqhat. In due course, the birth of the boy is celebrated for a full week by a feast in the family palace. The occasion is gladdened by the presence of the Kosharot, songstresses comparable with the muses. The Kosharot, who appear commonly in the Ugaritic poems, occur only once in the Bible (Psalm 68:7; 68:6 in the King James Bible), where the word "Kosharot" was not understood until after the discovery of the Ugaritic tablets.

When grown to a youth, Aqhat loses his life by antagonizing the goddess Anath. He is avenged by his sister Pughat (after whom the Hebrew heroine Puah is named in Exodus 1:15).[17] Before taking vengeance, Pughat dons male garb, girds a sword, and conceals the masculine attire and weapon by wearing a woman's dress over them. This circumstance provides an explanation of why the Bible forbids masquerading in the garb of the opposite sex; transvestism was abhorrent to the Hebrews precisely because it had an honored place in Canaanite culture.[18]

Danel curses the land on which Aqhat had been slain in the following words:

> Seven years may Baal afflict thee
> Eight, the Rider of Clouds!
> Let there be no dew
> Let there be no rain
> Let there be no surging of the Two Deeps
> Let there be no goodness of Baal's voice!

This brief passage is replete with biblical parallels. The phenomenon of the seven- (or climactically, eight-) year famine has been discussed. Baal's epithet, "Rider of Clouds," is applied to God in

---

[17] Hebrew *Pûʿā(h)* corresponds exactly to Ugaritic *Pûghat-*.

[18] Deuteronomy 22:5 reads, "The instrument of a male shall not be on a woman, nor shall a male wear the garb of a woman, for all who do these things are an abomination of Yahweh, thy God." This is usually taken nowadays to mean merely that men and women are to wear only the clothing appropriate to their sex. Josephus (*Antiquities* 4:301) paraphrases this law differently: "Beware especially in battles lest a woman use a male instrument, and lest a man wear a woman's dress." The original Hebrew (quite in keeping with Josephus's interpretation) seems indeed to prohibit also the use of any weapon by women. The fact that a sacred text of the pagan Ugaritians has Pughat wielding a man's sword, helps explain why the Hebrew reaction is so strong, using such emphatic language for what appears to the impartial observer as an impropriety rather than a crime.

Psalm 68:5; 68:4 in the King James Bible; the Ugaritic has clarified for all time the Hebrew word for "clouds" in this epithet. But most interesting of all is the fact that the curse reverberates in David's execration of Mount Gilboa (II Samuel 1:21), the place where Saul and Jonathan were slain:

> O mountains of Gilboa
> Let there be no rain
> Let there be no dew upon you!

Danel and David react in the same way and express themselves in almost identical words because the culture and literature of heroic Israel stemmed from the heritage of Canaan.

The extant fragments of the *Epic of Aqhat* do not preserve the part in which he is restored to life, but that he will be revived is anticipated in the text and required by the Hebrew allusions to the *Epic*.

Danel is described in the text as a ruler who dispenses judgment. He belongs to the governing class. The other Ugaritic epic also deals with a ruler, King Kret. The only heroes acceptable in the ancient East Mediterranean epic were kings (or at least kinglets) and other members of the ruling class. The Patriarchal Narratives of Genesis fit into this scheme, for Abraham and Sarah are plainly described as the founders of a royal line (Genesis 17:6, 16), and the circle in which they move is aristocratic. Socially, they deal with Pharaoh and the Philistine King of Gerar. Moreover, in role Abraham is a king, functioning as commander in chief of a coalition against another coalition of kings (Genesis 14).

We have, at present, three royal epics from Bronze Age Canaan: the two Ugaritic epics and the story of the Patriarchs. All three deal with the securing by divine aid of a special son through whom the royal line is continued. Furthermore, all three epics have a number of other fundamental threads in common.

Like Abraham and Daniel, King Kret is blessed with the special progeny only after incubation, sacrifices, and receipt of a divine promise.

The *Epic of Kret* is of prime importance because it bridges the gap between royal epic in Homer and in Genesis. It deals with a king (Kret) whose destined wife (Ḥurrai) has departed. He must therefore retrieve her from the palace of another king. This is essentially the Helen-of-Troy motif. Helen (like Ḥurrai) must be retrieved by her royal husband from the palace of another king. Not only these main lines, but innumerable details are shared by the *Epic of Kret* and the *Iliad*. Moreover, something else has emerged from the piling up of the *Kret* parallels with the *Iliad*, on the one hand, and with the Patriarchal Narratives in Genesis, on the other. It turns out that the Helen-of-Troy motif is prominent in Genesis, although until the discovery of the connecting link from Ugarit it went unnoticed. Sarah was taken away from her royal husband twice, once into the palace of Pharaoh and once into the palace of Abimelech (Genesis 12:10–20; 20:1–18). Both times she was retrieved by Abraham. Today an attempt would be made to hush up such a story; but in Mycenaean times, no East Mediterranean royal epic was complete without it.

The name of the hero Kret appears in the Bible. A brook bears his name in I Kings 17:3, 5. The same name is borne by the eponymous ancestor of the Cretans or the Philistines in Zephaniah 2:6.[19] It occurs commonly among the names in the Minoan tablets from Hagia Triada.

It should thus be apparent that Ugarit has the most intimate connections with the Old Testament in language and literature. At the same time, Ugarit has close Aegean connections. Through the Helen-of-Troy motif in the Epic of Kret, Ugaritic literature bridges the gap between the *Iliad* and Genesis.

---

[19] Written *krt*. Points like this can be studied only in the original Hebrew text.

Chapter III

MINOAN CRETE

Minoan civilization appeared suddenly on the island of Crete
with the period known to archaeologists as MM I (Middle Minoan
I). According to conventional chronology, that period began around
2000 B.C.; but there are reasons for reducing the date to about 1800
B.C. In any case, in MM I, the first Minoan palaces were built and
a pictographic syllabary was used to record the first real inscriptions, with sentence structure, ever written on European soil.

Evidently a strong wave of newcomers ushered in the new era
on Crete, for Minoan civilization made its debut there fully developed, without prior evolution on the island. There were, to be
sure, pre-Minoan people on Crete, but they had not gone beyond a
Neolithic stage of culture when the Minoan palace builders came.
The pre-Minoan Cretans had come from the mainland, some of
them from Anatolia. The Minoans themselves must have come from
the south, for their palaces have no built-in hearths to protect the
residents from the cold and raw days of a Cretan winter. Indeed,
the interiors were exposed to the elements by light-and-air wells,
thus aggravating the heating problem.

The southern clime whence the Minoan palace builders came is
not hard to determine. It must have been the Nile Delta, for Cretan
archaeology has yielded a host of artifacts imported from, or imi-
tating the workmanship of, Egypt. The creators of the ivory-and-
gold goddess figurines of Crete depended on Egypt for both materials; Crete itself had neither elephants nor any metal mines. Indeed, Minoan chronology is linked to Near East history mainly
through Egyptian scarabs and other Pharaonic inscriptions found
in the Cretan excavations. Genesis 10:13–14 correctly derives the

Cretans (called the "Philistines" and "Caphtorians") from Egypt.[1]

The interrelations between Egypt and Minoan Crete are well attested, but there is a great difference between Minoan and what we call Egyptian culture. This difference is largely due to the fact that most of what we know archaeologically about ancient Egypt comes from dry Upper Egypt and not from damp Lower Egypt. The two Egypts were rather different lands. Upper Egypt was the more distinctive and normally served as the center of nationalism. The Delta, on the other hand, was rather a part of the Mediterranean world, and many of its people were Semites and other non-Egyptians. In a sense, the Delta can be called the cradle of Western civilization because from it emerged the Minoans who founded the first high culture of Europe, and later the Hebrews of the Exodus, who migrated to their Promised Land. Thus the forerunners of classical Greek and Hebrew cultures were kindred Delta folk.

Minoan religion has close links with Canaan. For example, in MM I, natural mountain sanctuaries appear on Crete of a piece with the Canaanite high-places outlawed in the Bible. The West Semitic name for such mountain altars (*bom-o* [2] in Hebrew) has passed by way of Minoan into Greek as *bōm-ós*. Minoan temple-palaces have no idols, nor any place for installing them, for the official cult was aniconic. This avoidance of idols to represent the great god recalls the Re cult of Egypt. Though Egypt was highly idolatrous, the Re temples had been devoid of idols since Old Kingdom times. It is interesting to note that about twenty personal names in the Minoan tablets from HT (Hagia Triada) end in *-re;* some, perhaps most, of them are Egyptian names ending with the name of the god Re. Thus *ne-tu-ri-re* (HT 3:5) = Egyptian *ntry-r^c*,[3] "Re is divine"; *ra-na-re* (HT 47:b:1; 94:b:4; 62:2?) = Egyptian *rn-r^c*, "name of Re";

---

[1] Called to my attention by Dr. David Neiman.

[2] Each vowel (called a *qameṣ*) is meant to be pronounced *o*, as is reflected in various ancient records, and as is still perpetuated by the Ashkenazic Jews of eastern Europe.

[3] Postvocalically, laryngeals such as *^{c}* and *ḥ* lose their consonantal quality and color the preceding vowel in Minoan, much as in Akkadian. *Cf.* the weakening of laryngeals in Punic (Z. S. Harris, *A Grammar of the Phoenician Language,* Philadelphia, 1936, pp. 27–28). The development from classical Egyptian *Ra^c* to *Rê* is like that of *Ba^{c}l* to Akkadian *Bêl*.

a-ra-na-re (HT 1:a:4) = Egyptian *ᶜȝ-rn-rᶜ*, "great is the name of Re"; *pa-ya-re* (HT 8:b:4; 88:4; 117:a:5) = Egyptian *pȝy-rᶜ*, "man of Re" (literally, "he of Re"); and so on.

There can be little doubt that the later Hebrews also came under the influence of the Re cult and were thereby bolstered in their aversion to idols. Genesis 41:45, 50–51 tells us that Joseph married the daughter of the priest of Heliopolis (the center of the Re cult); she bore him his two sons, Manasseh and Ephraim. Moses married the daughter of Reuel, which may mean "Re is god" [4] (Exodus 2:18). A son of Naphtali is named Ahira (*'ᵃḥi-raᶜ*), "Re is brotherly" (Numbers 1:15)—a name formed quite like "Ahijah," "Yah(weh) is brotherly."

The widespread notion that the Minoans worshiped a mother goddess needs qualification. It is true that figurines of the goddess with bare breasts are found in Minoan Crete to the exclusion of idols of the male head of the pantheon. Yet the contradiction is apparent, not real. Officially, the chief god was male and aniconic. The popular religion, however, was geared to fertility and venerated the goddess of fertility. In Israel, we find much the same situation. We know from the Bible that the official deity was male and image-less, but the common people persisted in worshiping pagan deities such as the goddesses Asherah and Astarte. In Judean houses down to the destruction of the Temple in 586 B.C., we find Astarte images of the nude fertility goddess but no representations of God. We thus find comparable situations, *mutatis mutandis,* in both Crete and Israel: An aniconic male god is worshiped officially as the head of the pantheon; popular worship, however, emphasizes the idola-trous cult of the fertility goddess. If we had no Bible but only the information provided by Palestinian archaeology, we would think that Israelite religion was mainly the worship of Astarte. Now that we have begun to read the Minoan texts, we must (as we shall note below) revise our appraisal of Minoan religion.

Ancient tradition points plainly to the "Phoenician" (i.e., North-west Semitic) character of the Minoan language. Minos was the son of the Tyrian princess Europa. Her brother Cadmus founded

---

[4] Though "Friend of God" is also possible.

Thebes. "Europa" and "Cadmus" are an appropriate pair of Semitic names, meaning "West" and "East," respectively. The earliest recorded Greek tradition concerning the "Phoenicians" who introduced writing to Greece is from the logographer Hecataeus, who around 500 B.C. visited Egypt and wrote that Danaus (son of the Phoenician Belus and brother of Aegyptus) first brought writing to Greece. The Egyptian connections of Danaus are striking in the light of Minoan origins, for the weight of the evidence points to Delta Semites as the main stratum of the literate Minoan palace builders.

The knowledge that the Minoan language was "Phoenician" persisted until at least the fourth century A.D., when a Latin author, Lucius Septimius, described the accidental discovery of ancient literary texts at Knossos in the reign of Nero. The texts were brought to Nero, who assumed them to be Phoenician and turned them over to Semitists for translation. Arthur Evans, the father of Minoan archaeology, found the narrative by Septimius correct in its technical details (except, ironically, for the most important detail of all: the Phoenician identity of the language, which modern scholarship erroneously disfavored).[5]

The Minoan script is essentially a syllabary, whereby each sign stands for a consonant followed by a vowel. While it is not the normal system of Egypt, it operates like what is well known to Egyptologists as either "group-writing" or "syllabic orthography," used especially for Semitic words and names.[6] Minoan writing is pictographic in origin.[7] Its clearest and most beautiful pictorial form appears in the Phaistos Disk. However, other Minoan inscriptions also preserve a measure of the original pictorial nature of the script. A stone bowl from Gournes (near Apodulu) depicts the BIRD-OF-PREY and APPLE signs unmistakably.[8] Ventris, who

---

[5] A. J. Evans, *Scripta Minoa*, Vol. I, Oxford, 1909, p. 109.

[6] A. Gardiner, *Egyptian Grammar*, 3rd ed., London, 1957, p. 52 (§ 60).

[7] For comprehensive orientation, see M. Ventris and J. Chadwick, *Documents in Mycenaean Greek*, Cambridge, 1956. Maurice Pope gives additional bibliography in "Aegean Writing and Linear A," in *Studies in Mediterranean Archaeology*, Vol. VIII, Lund, 1964. I have described the decipherment of Minoan in *The Common Background of Greek and Hebrew Civilizations*, pp. 206–217, 300–303.

[8] The Minoan Linear A texts are published in the original script by W. C.

deciphered Mycenaean in 1952, determined the phonetic values of the Linear signs with no regard to their original pictographic form. In fact, he was not aware of the pictures underlying his Linear signs for *bu, ku, tu,* etc. which turn out to be MAN, BIRD-OF-PREY, APPLE, etc., respectively. We can now surmise the basis for the phonetic values of such signs. Each phonetic value is derived from the opening consonant + vowel of the word depicted, in Northwest Semitic, specifically in a dialect close to Ugaritic. The Ugaritic word for "man" is *bunushu,* whence MAN = *bu;* the Ugaritic word for BIRD-OF-PREY is *kudru,* whence BIRD-OF-PREY = *ku;* the Ugaritic word for "apple" is *tuppûhu,* whence APPLE = *tu.* This principle, known as acrophony, indicates that Minoan writing was invented for the Northwest Semitic language whose vocabulary provides the syllabic values for the signs that Ventris discovered cryptanalytically in complete ignorance of the Semitic language.

Two word groups on the Phaistos Disk suggest the following decipherment: BOAT-MOUTH-BARLEY-*ti* CORNER-MAN-*te*-BREAST-*da.* The syllables in small letters (*ti, te, da*) are based on graphic similarity to Linear signs whose values have been determined by Ventris. BOAT = *si* (from **sipinatu,* "boat"), MOUTH = *pe* (the word for "mouth" in Hebrew), BARLEY = *'i* (*cf.* Egyptian *it,* "barley"),[9] CORNER = *pi/bi* (from *pinnatu,* "corner," as in Hebrew), BREAST = *ha* (*cf.* Northwest Semitic *hayniq,* "to nurse"). The nine-sign sequence would therefore be read *si-pe-'i-ti bi-bu-te-ha-da,* "I have eaten (my ceremonial meal) in the temple of Hadd." Hadd is another name for Baal. The terminology is known from Ugaritic literature, for *spu ksmh bt b'l,* "one who eats his (ceremonial) meal in the house of Baal,"[10] is applied to a model son in the *Epic of Aqhat.* If this is correct, it seems that the Phaistos Disk is a ritual text associated with the Baal shrine in

Brice, *Inscriptions in the Minoan Linear Script of Class A,* London, 1961. The largest group of Linear A texts comes from Hagia Triada and has been republished in hand copy by G. Pugliese Carratelli, *Le Epigrafi de Haghia Triada in Lineare A* (Supplement 3 to *Minos*), Salamanca, 1963. The Gournes bowl is numbered "I,13" in Brice.

[9] Some Egyptian loanwords are to be expected.

[10] Ugaritic text 2 Aqhat I:32, which occurs in the *Epic of Aqhat,* translated below, in Chapter IV.

the royal palace.

The simplest way to understand the character of Minoan is to start not with the ancient pictographs on the Phaistos Disk, but rather with the latest form of Minoan (called "Eteocretan") in Greek letters on stone inscriptions from Crete between 600 and 300 B.C.

Two inscribed stones from Dreros, Crete, are bilingual, the first version being Eteocretan, the other, Greek. Since Greek is a known language it can serve as the key to the decipherment of the Eteocretan, assuming that the two versions are essentially the same text in translation. The Greek version of the first Dreros bilingual [11] ends in a dedicatory formula containing *matri*, "for mother." There is space for "his" which is now broken away. In any case the Eteocretan version ends in *lmo*, corresponding to Hebrew *l-immō*, "for his mother."

The second Dreros bilingual [12] evidently expresses a purification rite ending in the Greek version with *katharòn génoito*, "let there be purity." The last Greek word ("let there be") corresponds to *ihia*, the last word in the Eteocretan. Now *ihia* is the Minoan form of the verb "to be" that appears in Hebrew as *yihye*, "it will be," which can also function as the jussive "let there be." [13]

The Eteocretan unilinguals have so far come mainly from the Cretan town of Praisos. [14] The three best-preserved stones all have *mit*, "died," in the first line, suggesting that they are funerary. One of the formulas incorporated in these inscriptions apparently has the function of adjuring the passerby, whosoever he be, to deal kindly with the memory and interests of the deceased. One Praisos text expresses this in a ten-word phrase: *et me u mar krk o kl es u es*, "with whosoever he be, lord of the town or any man whosoever"; another Praisos text employs a variant wording: *nas iro u kl es*,

[11] In C. H. Gordon, "The Dreros Bilingual," *Journal of Semitic Studies*, 8, 1963, pp. 76–79.

[12] Republished by W. A. McDonald in "Note on a Fragment of an Archaic Inscription from Dreros," *Hesperia*, 25, 1956, pp. 69–72 and plate 27.

[13] See the discussion in C. H. Gordon, "The Decipherment of Minoan," *Natural History Magazine*, 72, no. 9, Nov. 1963, p. 29–30.

[14] The Praisos texts have been published on pp. 138–141 of Vol. III (1942) of M. Guarducci's *Inscriptiones Creticae*, Rome, 1935–50 (and to be continued).

"the people of his city and any man." The idea is the same in either wording; "everybody" is expressed by the combination of "fellow citizen" and "anyone else." Note that "lord of the town" and "people of his city" are synonymous in this idiom but their wordings are entirely different. Yet both are good Semitic

The most important Eteocretan text comes from Psychro,[15] where the sacred Dictaean Cave is located. The text is written in Greek letters, with the first word, *epithi,* repeated in Minoan syllabic signs: *'i-pi-ti.* Accordingly, the scribe knew the ancient syllabary as well as the newer alphabet. Moreover, two of the eighteen stone religious texts in Linear A come from the Dictaean Cave. It is at such famous shrines that old traditions tend to survive. The Eteocretan text from Psychro is fortunately a religious dedication that perpetuates some of the old Minoan terminology found in the eighteen known Linear A dedications, thereby proving that Eteocretan is a continuation of Minoan. In Minoan, *pi-ti* [16] means "engraved stone" (written *pṭḥ* in alphabetic Phoenician); Eteocretan *e-pithi* (with the definite article *e-*) means "the engraved stone." The Eteocretan text begins *epithi zēthanthē,* "the engraved stone which I have given," employing the verb (*y*)*atan,* "gave," that appears in Minoan dedications as well as in Phoenician and Ugaritic texts.

A cultic stone bowl from Apodulu [17] opens with the formula *ya-ta-no-x u ya-*[   ], "he has donated it and he has [set it up as a votive offering]," recalling the Phoenician formula *ytn w ytn',* "he has donated and set up as a votive offering." The first verb and the conjunction are the same in Minoan and in standard Phoenician. The Minoan form *u,* "and" (from original *wa*), is normal in Akkadian, Punic, and modern Arabic; it occurs sporadically in Ugaritic and under definable conditions in Hebrew.

There was a school of magic in the Semitic East that aimed at warding off demons through the use of incantation bowls inscribed

---

[15] First published by S. Marinatos in *Minoica* (Sundwall Festschrift), Berlin, 1958, pp. 226 ff.

[16] Minoan *pi-ti za* (for alphabetic Phoenician *pṭḥ z*), "this engraved stone," is inscribed on a stone libation table from Palaikastro (text I,4, in Brice). We have already noted the loss of postvocalic *ḥ* in Minoan.

[17] Text I,14, in Brice.

with ink and buried upside down in the buildings whose occupants wished to be protected. Most examples of this bowl magic come from Babylonia and adjacent areas for quite a few centuries before and after A.D. 500. The two earliest examples of such incantation bowls are, however, Minoan. They were found buried upside down under the floor at Knossos. The inscription on one of them [18] begins with the word *'a-ga-na,* "bowl," which is also used specifically to mean an incantation bowl in a magic text from Uruk.[19]

The largest collection of Minoan texts are the inventories on tablets from Hagia Triada. These are often called economic or administrative tablets. Some (perhaps most) of them are religious in that they record offerings to various gods. Some of the deities are familiar from the Canaanite pantheon: thus *'A-du* [20] (= Addu or Haddu, as Baal is sometimes called), *Gu-pà-nu* [21] (the vine god known from Ugaritic) and his female counterpart *Gu-pà-na-tu,*[22] *'A-ga-ru* [23] (the god of the field, called *Ugaru* in Ugaritic), *Ki-re-tá* [24] or *Ki-re-ta-na* [25] (called *Krt* or *Krtn* at Ugarit, where he is the divine king—son of the head of the pantheon, El, and the latter's consort, Asherah), *Ya-mo* [26] (the Northwest Semitic sea god Yamm), and *Ti-ni-ta* [27] (the Phoenician-Punic goddess called "our great Lady" and transliterated into Greek letters as *Thinith*). One of the foods offered is "wheat," spelled *ku-ni-su* [28] and followed by the WHEAT determinative.[29] In Linear B texts the same WHEAT determinative

[18] Text II,2, in Brice.

[19] For an introduction to the incantation bowls of Babylonia, see my *Adventures in the Nearest East,* London, 1957, pp. 160–174. The Uruk text is transliterated and translated in C. H. Gordon, "The Cuneiform Aramaic Incantation," *Orientalia,* 9, 1940, pp. 29–38.

[20] Receives offerings in seven HT (Hagia Triada) tablets: HT 85: a:1; 86:a:4; 88:1; 92:1; 95:b:1; 99:a:1; 133:1. The Ugaritic counterparts can be found in the "Glossary" of *UT,* which contains the proper names as well as the vocabulary words.

[21] HT 1:a:3; 3:6; 49:a:6–7; 88:3,4; 117:a:3; 122:a:6,7.

[22] HT 47:a:1–2; 119:3. *Cf. Gu-pà-na-tu-na* in I,13:b:1, in Brice.

[23] HT 2:1; 86:a:1; 86:b:1.

[24] HT 85:b:1–2; 129:1. Note the variant *Ki-ri-tá,* in HT 114:a:1; 121:1.

[25] HT 2:3; 8:a:5; 108:1; 120:4–5.

[26] HT 28:a:4; 28:b:1.

[27] HT 27:a:1.

[28] HT 10:a:1; 95:a:3; 95:b:3.

[29] HT 86:a:1–2; 86:b:1–2.

is sometimes accompanied by *si-to*, a Greek word (*sîtos*) that can designate wheat. The Minoan word *ku-ni-su* appears in Akkadian (as *kunnishu*) and in Aramaic (*kunniṭ-*) to designate kinds of wheat, such as emmer or spelt. The Linear A and B values of WHEAT thus provide us with the equation *ku-ni-su* = *si-to*, constituting a quasi-bilingual, confirming the Semitic character of the Linear A language.

There are Semitic names, including *Da-we-da*, "David," in the HT tablets.[30] As we have pointed out, there are also Egyptian names. Two of the HT names are Hurrian (*Da-ku-se-né*[31] and *Su-ki-ri-te-se-ya*[32]), pointing to a Hurrian segment of the Minoan population. Canaan also gives us good documentation for the Hurrian segment of Semitic communities like Ugarit and Alalakh, where many of the people have pure Hurrian names. The Hurrians on Crete are of special interest to us because their presence explains how the Hurrian theogony (known as the Kumarbi Myth) reached the Greeks. Hesiod cites the Kumarbi Myth in Greek dress and localizes it at Lyktos, on Crete.[33] Accordingly Hesiod did not borrow the myth from Asia; it had been brought by Hurrians to Greek soil in the Bronze Age, long before his time.

We know for certain that the Cretan syllabary was not limited to one language. Linear A and B are in entirely different languages. It is possible that the same script was used for still other languages, such as Hurrian and Egyptian. However, this possibility should not obscure the fact that the main pre-Greek language of Crete, which we call "Minoan," is Northwest Semitic of a type called "Phoenician" by the ancient Hellenes. The Minoan pantheon is Northwest Semitic, and the widely distributed cultic texts are in one and the same Northwest Semitic language which persisted on Crete into Hellenistic times, when it was still sometimes written in the old syllabary, though more often in what we call Greek letters.

Our knowledge of Minoan vocabulary, grammar, and syntax is

[30] HT 10:a:5; 85:a:2; 93:a:7; 122:a:7.
[31] HT 103:2–3,4–5. *Cf.* what may be the Semitized feminine form *Da-ku-se-né-ti* in HT 104:1–2.
[32] II,7:b, in Brice.
[33] *Theogony*, 477–482. See the discussion in *The Common Background of Greek and Hebrew Civilizations*, pp. 92–93.

such that we are not limited to nouns that might be isolated loan-words.[34] We know four Semitic words for various metal or ceramic vessels in Minoan; [35] in the HT texts the Semitic *ku-lo*,[36] meaning "all," introduces totals; Semitic words for "wine" [37] and "wheat" occur in Minoan. If our Minoan vocabulary were limited to such words, it might be argued that they were cultural loanwords. How-ever, a group of Semitic nouns, such as "mother," "man," "people," "town," and "city" [38] are not likely to be borrowings. The Minoan verbs "to be," "to give or donate," and "to set up as an offering"; the Minoan pronouns "he," "his," "this," and "all"; the Minoan con-junctions "and" and "or"; the Minoan numerals "seven," "nine," and "ten"; [39] the Minoan preposition "to, for," are all Northwest Semitic and cannot be loanwords. Moreover, the grammar and syntax are Semitic, so that the Northwest Semitic nature of Minoan is estab-lished by the primary evidence.

Ugarit and Minoan Crete belonged to the same Northwest Semitic

[34] I presented the first methodical sketch of the language under the title of "Toward a Grammar of Minoan," in *Orientalia*, 32, 1963, pp. 292–297. A more detailed study, called *Evidence for the Minoan Language* will be published soon.

[35] No less than three Semitic vase names are spelled out phonetically and ac-companied by vase pictographs on HT 31. A fourth (*'a-ga-nu*) has been dis-cussed above.

[36] This word occurs thirty-three times in HT (e.g., 9:a:6; 9:b:6; 11:a:3). All Minoan words and names are indexed with text references (but only in the Minoan script, without transliteration or translation) in the "Vocabulary" at the end of Brice's book. (In using the latter, the reader must bear in mind that Brice has not distinguished the *ri* and *we* signs, nor the *'i* and *no* signs.) Students who have not yet learned the Minoan script may use the older but still useful monograph of P. Meriggi, *Primi Elementi di Minoica A*, Sala-manca, 1956, with regular and rhyming indices, in Latin letters, of the Minoan words and names, with text references.

[37] In accordance with orthographic rules established for Linear B, *ya-ne* can represent Northwest Semitic *yain-*, "wine" (like *a-na-ta* for *a-na-i-ta* in Ventris and Chadwick, p. 43). Note that *ya-ne* is incised on a fragment of a large wine jar from Knossos (text II,3, in Brice); other similar jars from Knossos are marked with the WINE ideogram (texts II,5; II,6:ii,iii; in Brice).

[38] These words occur in the Eteocretan passages discussed above. We may also note that a Northwest Semitic word for "city" occurs on a Minoan libation table (text I,3, in Brice) from Palaikastro: *k[i]-re-ya-tu* = *qryt*, "city," in Ugaritic, Hebrew, and other Northwest Semitic dialects.

[39] So far, these numerals are attested only in Eteocretan; see my edition of the Praisos and Psychro texts, with translations of intelligible passages, in "Eteo-cretan," *Journal of Near Eastern Studies*, 21, 1962, pp. 211–214.

sphere linguistically, religiously, and culturally. Geographically, they fitted into the same East Mediterranean region. Chronologically, their histories overlapped. Ugarit had developed its cuneiform alphabet prior to the great impact of the Minoans on Ugarit shortly after 1400 B.C. It was then that Ugaritic literature suddenly flowered, looking back to Crete as the homeland of its arts.

We have rich literary remains from Ugarit, but little so far from Minoan Crete. This is due to the accidents of discovery. Sooner or later we may have real literary texts from the Minoans. Meanwhile the known Minoan texts suffice to bridge the gap between Ugarit and Greece, and show us that Northwest Semites laid the Minoan foundations for Mycenaean civilization: the first Greek culture in recorded history.

Chapter IV

UGARITIC POETRY

Ugaritic poetry may be divided into two main categories: myth and epic. These terms must be defined because they are used differently by different authors. By a "myth" we mean here a narrative aimed at explaining either a natural phenomenon, such as some basic aspect of fertility (e.g., rain or dew), or a general condition affecting man's welfare (e.g., peace, health, or prosperity). The myth can be used in religion to induce well-being by sympathetic principles. For instance, the myth of Baal's triumph over Mot was invoked to bring on fertility for his devotees. Ritual drama reenacts myth so as to reproduce the beneficial effect attributed to the myth.

"Epic" is the term we shall apply to heroic narratives about people, although the gods are constantly affecting their destiny. The heroes and heroines of the epics are of the ruling class; the epic is not concerned with common people. Continuity of the royal line is of prime interest. The nobility of the crown prince's mother is important because a noble scion should preferably be of noble parentage on both sides, even though paternity (and not maternity) is the determining factor of class membership in a patriarchal society. The people worthy of a place in the epic are greater than life-size. As such they mingle with the gods socially. El is among the guests at King Kret's homecoming with Queen Ḥurrai. Epics often have a historical kernel; myths are usually devoid of any historical basis.

Both the myths and the epics of Ugarit are written in poetry. The structure of the poetry consists of parallelistic balance, in which two or more units of expression repeat, oppose, or otherwise complement each other. The language of poetry has many words, phrases,

and epithets of its own. Synonymous words and whole expressions
are necessitated by parallelism, for the very nature of the poetry
requires repetition in different phraseology. If "Baal" is mentioned
in one hemistich, the poet can call him "Hadd" or "Dagon's Son" or
"the Rider of Clouds" (depending on the length of phrase desired)
in the parallel hemistich. There is no requirement to adhere to the
same cadence throughout an entire poem. The large variety of traditional cadences offers so many possible combinations of verses and
stanzas that Ugaritic (like Hebrew) poetry has much more struc-
tural vivacity than dactylic hexameter can provide. There is no need
to illustrate the metric variety within any given Ugaritic poem,
because the nature of the original Ugaritic (at least its parallelism)
carries over into the English translation and can be observed below
in this chapter.[1]

A large group of texts deal with myths pertaining to Baal and
Anath. They can best be discussed in some sequence that supplies
a meaningful continuity, provided that we understand that the
sequence is ours, and that it has not been prescribed by the poets or
priests of Ugarit.[2] We start with text 129, which tells of the sea god,
Yamm, who on winning kingship, has a palace built for him by
Kothar-and-Ḥasis. We begin with this fragment because Yamm's
kingship and palace precede Baal's, as will appear later.[3]

[   ] father [   ]   (129:1

  [   ] to [   ]

[Thereupon] he sets face toward El

At the sources [of the Two Rivers]

  [In the midst of the streams of the Two Deeps].

[He enters] the abode of El   (5

---

[1] For an analysis of the varieties of Ugaritic prosody with reference to verbal
composition, parallelism, and bulk, see *UT*, pp. 130–144.

[2] A. Herdner groups the texts somewhat differently in her *Corpus des tablettes
en cunéiformes alphabétiques*, Paris, 1963.

[3] In the following translations, words missing or broken away on the tablets
are put between brackets. Italics are used to indicate very doubtful translations.
Dashes indicate passages which are still untranslatable. The single, double, and
triple lines in the texts were drawn by the scribes to mark off sections of the
tablets. Words added in translation are in parentheses. The numbers on the right
margins refer to the edition of the Ugaritic texts in *UT*.

And comes into the domicile of the King, [Father of Šnm [4]].
[At the feet of El he bows] and falls
    Prostrates himself and honors [him].
[   ]
Kothar-and-Ḫa[sis   ] house of Sea
    [   ] palace of Judge River.
Thy bosom [   ]
Build the house of Prince Sea
    [Ere]ct the pala[ce of Judge] River
In the midst of [   ]
    [   ] build [   ]   (:10
    [   ] erect [   ]
[   ]
[   ] lad to the fields, words
[   ] in the sea.
Sea [   ] Athtar of [   ]
[   ] fire
[   ] bring [   ] son(s)
[   ] the Luminary of the Gods, Sun.   (:15
She lifts her voice
    And [shouts]:
"[Hea]r! – – – –
Thor-El,[5] thy father, [   ]
To the presence of Prince Sea
    [Judge Riv]er
Will not Thor-El, thy father, hear thee?
    Will he not remove [the props of thy throne]?

---

[4] Šnm is a deity sired by El. He appears in ritual texts fused with T̲kmn, in the combination T̲kmn-w-Šnm.

[5] T̲ôr (pronounced "T̲ôr"), "the Bull," is identified with El, the head of the pantheon. Israel officially accepted El as the one and only God, but it experienced difficulty in purging the cult of El of its old theriomorphic traits. It was all right for the Greeks to envisage Zeus as a bull carrying off Europa, but the Bible could not sanction the representation of God in such a form. Yet the biblical record unmistakably shows that when Israel lapsed into its old pagan patterns, it fell back repeatedly into bull and calf worship as we have noted above. Hebrew religion officially reacted against cults of Canaan and Crete, but for a long time Israel did not embrace incorporeal monotheism without some survivals and revivals of anthropomorphism and theriomorphism. It was hard for Israel to divest itself of bull worship precisely because El (who was accepted as the one and only God) had long been identified with the Bull, as we now see from the Ugaritic myths.

[Nor up]set [the chair] of thy kingship?
    Nor break the scepter of thy government?"
And [   ] replies:
"[   ] against me, Thor-El, my father.
As for me, [I have] no house [like] the gods
    Nor a court [like the deiti]es!   (:20
To the *womb*, I'll descend
    When I'm reborn the Kothars will wash me
In the hou[se] of Sea
    In the palace of Judge River."
Thor-El, his father, – – – –, Judge [   ]:
"[Judg]e River, thou art King!
    [   ] mayest thou reign!
Lo, there is no wife, [   ] like
[   ] Prince Sea
    [   ] Judge River
[   ] he will send me."
And Athtar replies: [   ]

Text 137 tells of Yamm's demand that Baal be turned over to him. Yamm makes his arrogant request through messengers sent to the convocation of the gods under the presidency of El. Baal, though infuriated by Yamm's insolence, is handed over by El as a slave to Yamm.

[   ]   (137:1
"Thou has arisen against [   ]"
[And] Aliyan Baal [replies]:
"[   ]   (:5
On thy head, Aymr [   ]
    [On thy pate Ygrš [6]   ]!"
[And] Judge River [replies]:
"May [Horon] break, [O Baal]!
    [May Horon break] thy head
        Astarte-[Name-of Baal, thy pate]!"
[   ] Staff fall in By[blos   ]
[   ] two women [   ]   (:10
[me]ssengers sends Sea [   ]

[6] Aymr ("Driver") and Ygrš ("Expeller") are the names of war clubs fashioned by Kothar-and-Ḥasis. The first stuns the foe; the second vanquishes him. These clubs are mentioned in text 68, below.

in – – – – – – – – – fowl [   ]
– – – break also they.
"Depart, lad[s]!
  [Do not sit!]
[Then] ye shall surely set [face]
Toward the Convocation of the Assembly
  In the mi[dst of the mountain of Night].
[At the feet of El] do not fall   (:15
  Do not prostrate yourselves before the Convocation [of the Assembly]
But declare your information!
And say to Thor, [my] father, [El]!
  [Declare to the Convocation] of the Assembly:
'The message of Sea, your lord,
  Of your master Ju[dge River]:
"Give up, O gods, him whom you harbor
  Him whom the multitude harbor!
Give up Baal [and his partisans]
  Dagon's Son, so that I may inherit his gold!" ' "
The lads depart
  They do not sit.
[Then] they set [face]   (:20
Toward the mountain of Night
  Toward the Convocation of the Assembly.
The gods had not even sat down
  The deities to dine,
When Baal stood up by El.
As soon as the gods saw them
  Saw the messengers of Sea
    The emissaries of Judge River
The gods lowered their heads upon their knees
  Yea upon the thrones of their lordships.
Baal rebukes them:
"Why, O gods, have ye lowered
  Your heads on top of your knees   (:25
    Yea upon the thrones of your lordships?
Let a pair [7] of gods read

---

[7] Apparently the gods who could read were a pair of divine scribes, even as
the divine messengers (and many other deities) came in pairs. See *UT* § 19.126
for *aḥd* (*m*), "pair"; the common meaning of "one" is ruled out by the
dual/plural verb here.

The tablets of the messengers of Sea
  Of the emissaries of Judge River!
O gods, lift up your heads
  From the top of your knees
    Yea from the thrones of your lordships!
And I shall answer
The messengers of Sea
  The emissaries of Judge River."
The gods lift their heads
  From on top of their knees
    Yea from the thrones of their lordships.
After there arrive the messengers of Sea   (:30
  The emissaries of Judge River
At the feet of El they do [not] fall
  They do not prostrate themselves before the Convocation of the Assembly.
Arise [   ] they declare their information.
A fire, two fires!
  He sees a burnished sword!
[   ] them.
They say to Thor, his father, El
"The message of Sea, your lord,
  Of your master, Judge River:
'Give up, O gods, him whom ye harbor
  Him whom the [multitudes] harbor!   (:35
Give up Baal and his partisans
  Dagon's Son, so that I may inherit his gold!' "
[And] Thor, his father, El, [replies]:
"Baal is thy slave, O Sea!
  Baal is thy slave, [O S]ea!
    Dagon's Son is thy captive!
He will bring thy tribute like the gods
  He will bring [   ]
    Like the deities, thy gift!"
But Prince Baal is infuriated.
[A knife he tak]es in the hand
  A dagger in the right hand.
To smite the lads [8] he flo[urishes them/it].

  [8] I.e., the two messengers of Sea.

[Ana]th seizes [his right hand]   (:40
  Astarte seizes his left hand:
"How [canst thou smite the messengers of Sea],
  [The emis]saries of Judge River?
The messengers – – – – – – [   ]
[   ] messengers on the shoulders
Word of his lord and [   ]"
But Prince Baal is infuriated.
Fields in [   ]
The messengers of Sea
  The [emis]saries of Judge Riv[er   ]   (:45
I have spoken to Sea, your lord,
  [Your] ma[ster, Judge River].
Gmr-Hadd – – – [   ]
[   ] bow down [   ]

    Text 68 relates how Baal vanquishes Yamm and drives him from his
sovereignty through the use of two magic clubs fashioned by Kothar-and-
Ḥasis for this particular battle.

[   ] dead [   ]   (68:1
[   ] alive [   ]
I shall bring them out
  Also I shall drive out [   ]
[   ] and in the sea – – – – – –
  In the sea two bosoms [   ]
[Judge] River – – – – there two swords – – – – – I shall kiss [   ] (:5
"To the earth let *our* mighty one fall
  Yea to the dust, *our* strong one."
[From] his mouth the word had not yet gone forth
  Nor from his lips, his utterance
And his voice was given forth
Like a mountain under the throne of Prince Sea.
And Kothar-and-Ḥasis declared:
"Did I not tell thee, O Prince Baal,
  Nor declare, O Rider of Clouds?
'Lo, thine enemies, O Baal,
  Lo, thine enemies wilt thou smite
    Lo, thou wilt vanquish thy foes

Thou wilt take thine eternal kingdom   (:10
   Thine everlasting sovereignty!' "
Kothar brings down two clubs
   And proclaims their names.
"Thy name, even thine, is Expeller!
Expeller, expel Sea
   Expel Sea from his throne
      River from the seat of his sovereignty!
Thou shalt swoop from the hands of Baal
   Like an eagle from his fingers!
Strike the shoulders of Prince Sea
   'Twixt the hands of [Jud]ge River!"   (:15
The club swoops from the hands of Baal
   Like an eagle from his fingers.
It strikes the shoulders of Prince Sea
   'Twixt the hands of Judge River.
Sea is strong
   He is not vanquished
His joints do not fail
   Nor his frame collapse.
Kothar brings down two clubs
   And proclaims their names.
"Thy name, even thine, is Driver!
Driver, drive Sea
   Drive Sea from his throne   (:20
      River from the seat of his sovereignty!
Thou shalt swoop from the hands of Baal
   Like an eagle from his fingers!
Strike the head of Prince Sea
   'Twixt the eyes of Judge River!
Let Sea sink
   And fall to earth!"
And the club swoops from the hands of Baal
   Like an eagle from his fingers.
It strikes the head of Prince [Sea]   (:25
   'Twixt the eyes of Judge River.
Sea sinks
   Falls to earth
His joints fail

His frame collapses
Baal drags and poises Sea
    Destroys Judge River.
By name, Astarte rebukes:
"Shame, O Aliyan Baal,
    Shame, O Rider of Clouds!
For Prince Sea was our captive
    For Judge River was our captive."   (:30
And there went out B[aal   ]
    Verily ashamed is Aliyan Baal
And [Prince] Sea is indeed dead
    So let Baal rei[gn]!
Heat [9] for the – – – – – and [and]
says: "Sea is dead"
for – – – – and she answ[ers   ]   (:35
those lords [   ]
for the – – – [   ]
in his head [   ]
[   ]
[   ] his eyes [   ]

The Anath text refers, in column I, to a divine banquet with abundant
wine and a minstrel who sings to the accompaniment of cymbals. Column II tells of how Anath's bloodthirsty rampage nearly destroys all of
mankind; the massacre found a place in the sacred literature because it
symbolizes victory and ends on a note of the blessings of peace that
follow victory. Columns III–IV tell how Baal induces Anath to visit him
on his holy mountain by promising to reveal to her the secret of nature.
She at first fears that the invitation is prompted by some danger threaten-
ing Baal, and assures the messengers of Baal who bring the invitation
that she is willing to take on any foe of Baal, even as she has vanquished
foes of his in the past, to wit, Yamm ("Sea"), Tannin (the dragon Leviathan), Mot ("Death"), and so on. Baal's messengers, Gupan and Ugar,
assure her that there is no trouble, but that she should make certain offerings and hasten to Baal, who will reveal his great secret. She obeys and
brings with her the blessings of rain, dew, game, and fish.

Actually Baal's aim is to get Anath to set in motion his request for a

---

[9] The heat is apparently destructive heat that withers crops. When a god or
hero is slain, nature responds by languishing.

palace. Columns IV–V narrate how Anath extorts by threats of violence El's permission to build the palace. Column VI refers to the delegation sent to Kothar-and-Ḥasis with Baal's request that the Caphtorian god build it.[10]

The Anath text closes with a parallel section (duplicating scenes of the offering) and then with a mission to Kothar-and-Ḥasis (with the request that he come to learn the secret of nature). An additional fragment closes with a ceremony in which El proclaims some divine names at a feast in connection with the construction of a palace.

"Do not lower [   ]   (ʿnt:I:1 [11]
Serve Aliyan Baal
   Honor the Prince, Lord of Earth."
He proceeded to prepare (a repast)
   So that he might feed him.   (:5
He put a breast before him
With a keen knife
   A slice of fatling.
He began to prepare beverages
   So as to give him to drink.
He set a cup in his hand   (:10
   A goblet in both his hands.
From the mighty *cherub* we – – – – –.
The men of heaven saw not the sacred cup
   The women of the goblet eyed not Asherah.   (:15
A thousand pitchers he took from the wine
   A myriad he mixed with its mixture.
He proceeded to sing and chant

---

[10] As we have noted above, the myth harks back to the time when Caphtor was the hub of the Northwest Semitic world in Minoan times. When the Mycenaean Greeks conquered the Minoan sphere, the Northwest Semitic sea lords were forced to center their sphere on the Syro-Palestinian coast, at places like Tyre, Sidon, Byblos, Arwad, and Ugarit. Accordingly, in the tenth century B.C., Solomon turned to Tyre for aid in building Yahweh's Temple, even as Ugarit had looked to Caphtor. It is interesting to note that (in accordance with the requirements of monotheism) God absorbed the roles of the various gods in the old pantheon, including Kothar-and-Ḥasis' role. Note that I Chronicles 28:19 ascribes the plan of Solomon's Temple to Yahweh's architectural design, written in Yahweh's own handwriting. Earlier (*ca.* 2000 B.C.) the Sumerian ruler Gudea of Lagash claimed (in his Cylinder A, col. VI:3–5) that the god Nindub had brought him the plan for building the Eninnu temple.

[11] ʿnt is the Ugaritic spelling for Anath.

With cymbals in the hands of the Good One
    The lad, good of voice, sang   (:20
        About Baal in the heights of Saphon.
Baal views his girls
    He sees Pidray, girl of light
        Also Ṭallay, [girl] of rain   (:25
(*four lines missing*)
Like the fruit of seven daughters   (:II:2
The scent of kids and *anhb*-animals
Both gates of Anath's house.[12]
And the lads chance upon the Lady of the Mountain   (:5
And lo Anath smites in the valley [13]
    Fighting between the two cities
She smites the people of the s[ea]shore
    Destroys mankind of the sunrise.[14]
Under her are heads like vultures
    Over her are hands like locusts [15]   (:10
        Like thorns of *ġrmn*, the hands of troops.
She piles up heads on her back
    She ties up hands in her bundle.
Knee-deep she plunges in the blood of soldiery
    Up to the neck in the gore of troops.   (:15
With a stick she drives out foes
    Against the flank she draws her bow.
And lo Anath reaches her house
    Yea the goddess enters her palace
But is not satisfied.
She had smitten *it* in the valley
Fought between the two cities.   (:20

---

[12] The consonantal text permits such a translation. However, the sequence of phrases makes no sense and therefore can not be entirely correct. No part of the translation has been marked as doubtful because each word *by itself* is definable. The difficulty hinges on the lack of vowels, which generally makes it possible for any word, taken *by itself*, to have several different pronunciations and meanings. Certainty of translation comes with clarity of context, which is lacking here, partly due to the preceding lacuna in the tablet.

[13] The text has b^emq, which can mean either "in the valley" or "violently."

[14] The pair of opposites (seashore = west, and sunrise = east) indicates totality, as antonymic pairs frequently do. The meaning is that Anath is decimating all of mankind.

[15] I.e., the air is full of the heads and hands she is hacking off her victims.

She hurls chairs at the troops
  Hurling tables at the soldiers
    Footstools at the heroes.
Much she smites and looks
  Fights and views.
Anath gluts her liver with laughter   (:25
  Her heart is filled with joy
    For in Anath's hand is victory.
For knee-deep she plunges in the blood of soldiery
  Up to the neck in the gore of troops.
Until she is sated [16] she smites in the house
  Fights between the two tables   (:30
Shedding – – – – the blood of soldiery
  Pouring the oil of peace from a bowl.
The Virgin Anath washes her hands.
    The Progenitress of Heroes,[17] her fingers.
She washes her hands in the blood of soldiery
  Her fingers in the gore of troops.   (:35
[Arran]ging portions by the chairs
  Tables by the table(s)

---

[16] Note that the style calls for duplicating the battle scene. In line 19 above it is stated that Anath was not satisfied with the bloodshed in the first foray. Accordingly she sallied forth on another battle and this time she was satisfied. This feature of the literature is of the greatest importance in understanding Hebrew and Greek literatures. The usual approach to such duplications is to assume that two sources have been combined by a later editor. For example, in Judges 21, it is generally held that two separate stories, from different sources, tell how the decimated Benjaminites captured wives, first from Jabesh-Gilead and then from Shiloh, to assure the survival of the Tribe. That both incidents belong together is indicated by the statement that after capturing the girls from Jabesh-Gilead, the Benjaminites had still not found enough wives (v. 14), whereupon they captured more girls from Shiloh and so found the requisite number of wives (v. 23). As long as the Bible was approached mainly from the standpoint of a theory of documentary analysis, it appeared reasonable enough to assume that two sources had been clumsily stitched together. Ugaritic literature shows that the ancient style calls for the climactic parallelism of the two scenes; we are not dealing with a casual editor who conflated a "Jabesh-Gilead source" with a "Shiloh source." The Jabesh-Gilead and Shiloh scenes are two halves of one whole. The first is the prelude, the second, the climax. Neither half is, or ever was, a separate entity.

[17] This epithet of Anath (*ybmt limm*) is not yet clear. "Widowed Sister-in-Law of Nations" has also been suggested on the basis of Hebrew cognates. Our present interpretation is prompted by the fact that Anath was regarded as the mother of certain warriors (*cf.* Judges 3:31; 5:6).

Footstools she arranges by the footstools.
She gathers water and washes
    With dew of heaven
        Fat of Earth
            Rain of the Rider of Clouds
The dew that the heavens pour
    [The rain] that the stars pour.
The *anhb*-animals *leap* [by the thousand acres]
    The *ẓuh*-fish in the sea, [by the myriad of hectares].[18]
[   ]
"[   ]   (:III:1
Place corals on her chest *as a gift*
For the love of Aliyan Baal
    The affection of Pidray, girl of light,
        The devotion of Ṭallay, girl of rain,
            The love of Arṣay, girl of Yᶜbdr.   (:5
Like lads and [harbin]ger(s)
At Anath's feet bow and fall
    Prostrate yourselves, honor her
And say to the Virgin Anath
    Declare to the Progenitress of Heroes:
'The message of Aliyan Baal   (:10
    The word of Aliy the Warrior:
"Put bread in the earth
    Place mandrakes in the dust
Pour a peace offering in the midst of the earth
    A *libation* in the midst of the fields!
Thy *ḥš*   (:15
    Thy tree(s)
        Thy ᶜbṣ.[19]
To me let thy feet run
    To me let thy legs *hasten*.
For I have a word that I'll tell thee
    A matter that I'll declare to thee
'Tis the word of the tree   (:20

[18] The victory of Anath results in dew and rain, fertility of the soil, and abundance of game and fish. The main goal of this mythological literature is to secure life and fertility and to avert death and sterility.

[19] These three articles are Anath's symbols or insignia, which she carries with her. Other gods have different triple insignia.

Yea the whisper of the stone
  The murmur of the heavens to the earth
    Of the deeps to the stars.
I understand the lightning which the heavens do not know
  A matter that men do not know
    Nor the multitudes of the earth understand.   (:25
Come and I shall show it
In the midst of the mountain of me, god of Saphon, in the sanctuary
  In the mountain of mine inheritance, in the good place
    In the Hill of Power." ' "

As soon as Anath sees the gods,
On it the feet stamp   (:30
  On the plain she breaks the back
Above, her face sweats
  The joints of her back fail
    Her vertebrae are agitated.
She lifts her voice
  And shouts:
"Why have Gupan and Ugar come?
What enemy has arisen against Baal
  Or foe against the Rider of Clouds?   (:35
Did I not crush El's Darling, Sea?
  Nor destroy River, the great god?
    Nor muzzle Tannin full well?
I crushed the crooked serpent
  The mighty one of seven heads.
I crushed the darling of the earth gods   (:40
  Even Mot, the calf of El, – – –
I crushed Fire, the bitch of the gods
  I destroyed the daughter of the El-Zebub
I fought and got the gold
Of the one who drove out Baal from the heights of Saphon   (:IV:45
  Ousting like a bird of – – – – –
    Who drove him out from the seat of his kingship
      From the dais, from the throne of his sovereignty.
What enemy has arisen against Baal
  Or foe against the Rider of Clouds?"

And the lads indeed reply:
"No enemy has risen against Baal   (:50
  Nor foe against the Rider of Clouds.
(Here is) the message of Aliyan Baal
  The word of Aliy the Warrior:
'Put bread in the earth
  Set mandrakes in the dust
Pour a peace offering in the midst of the earth
  A *libation* in the midst of the fields!
Thy ḥš   (:55
  Thy tree(s)
    Thy ᶜbṣ
Unto me let thy feet run
  Unto me let thy legs *hasten!*
[For I have a word] that I'll tell thee
  A matter [that I'll declare to thee]
[The word] of the tree
  The whisper [of the stone]
[A word] that me[n do not kn]ow
  Nor the [multitudes of the ea]rth understand.   (:60
The murmur of the heavens to [the earth]
  Of the deeps [to the stars].
I understand lightning that the [heav]ens do not [know].
[Come and I] shall sh[ow it]
[In the midst of the moun]tain of me, god of Saphon, in the sanct[uary]
  In [the mountain] of mine [in]heritance.'"
And the Virgin Anath replies   (:65
  [The Progenitress] of heroes [responds]:
"I shall put bread [in the earth]
  [I shall] set mand[rakes] in the dust
I shall pour [a peace offering] in the midst of the earth
  A lib[ation] in the mids[t of the fi]elds.
Let him set [   ] Baal his *thunderbolts* flash   (:70
[   ]
I shall put bread in the earth
  I shall set mandrakes [in the] dust
I shall pour a peace offering in the midst of the earth
  A libation in the midst of the f[ields].   (:75
Also another matter I would tell,

Go! Go! O retainers of the gods
Ye are slow
   But I am fast!
Uǵar is not distant, O gods!
   Inbb is not distant, O deities!
Two *stages* under the springs of the earth   (:80
   Three *marches* (aloft in) the *hills*."
Thereupon she sets face toward the Lord of Saphon's crest.
By the thousand acres
   Myriad of hectares,
Baal sees the going of his sister
   Yea the course of his father's daughter.
He sends away women to her presence
   Setting an ox before her   (:85
      A fatling before her face.
She gathers her water
   That she may wash
With dew of heaven
   Fat of earth
The dew that the heavens pour
   The rain that the stars pour.
The *anhb*-animals *leap* by the thousand acres
   [The *ẓuh*-fish in the sea by the myriad of hectares].[20]   (:90
[   ]
"[Baal has no house like the gods]
   [Nor a court] like the sons of Asherah: (pl. vi:IV:1
The dwelling of El
   The shelter of his sons
      The dw[elling of Lady Asherah of the Sea],
The dwelling of Pidra[y, girl of light],
   [The shelter] of Ṭallay, girl of r[ain],
      [The dwelling of Arṣay], girl of Yᶜbdr.
[The dwelling of the] renowned [brides]."

---

[20] The fact that this scene is a repetition of what has appeared in another context above in column II is another one of the many reminders that repetitions (of various kinds) are characteristic of the literature. Inasmuch as the assumption that repetitions imply conflation is the cornerstone of standard documentary criticism, we see that the cornerstone is illusory. Repetitions (with varying differences in wording) are part and parcel of the literary style; in general they do not result from the combining of different sources.

And [the Virgin Anath] replies:
"Thor-El, [my father], will reconsider
  Reconsider for my sake and his
[Lest I] trample him like a lamb to the earth
  [Make] his gray hair [run] with blood   (:V:10
    The gray of his beard [with gore]
Unless a house be given to Baal like the gods
  [Yea a cour]t like the sons of Asherah."
[She springs with f]oot
  [And leaves] the earth.
Thereupon [she sets f]ace [toward El]
At the sources of the Two Rivers
  [The mid]st of the st[rea]ms of the Two [Deep]s.
She enters the abode of El
  Comes into the [domic]ile of the King, Father of [šnm].
The territory [   ] – – –
  The premises [   ] lord [   ]
Her voice is given [forth to] Thor-El, her father, [   ]
In the seven rooms
  [In the e]ight [cha]mbers [21] [   ]   (:20
Thor[-El] replied [   ]
Above [   ]
At the feet of the lads [   ]
Much [   ]
The Luminary of the Gods, Sun, [burn]s   (:25
  The heavens stop on [account of the god Mo]t.[22]
And the Virgin Anath replies:
"[   ] O gods [   ]
Do [not re]joice!
  Do not rejoice! [   ]
    Be not glad – – – [   ]   (:30
      In the greatness of – – – – –
[   ] thy head.
I shall make [thy] gray hair run [with blood]

[21] Anath is to threaten her aged father, El, with bodily violence so that he
hides in the innermost chamber (the eighth chamber-within-a-chamber). In-
timidated by his impetuous daughter, El will grant her demand that he
authorize the building of a palace for Baal.

[22] The stopping of the heavenly bodies is familiar from Joshua 10:12–13.

The gray of thy beard with gore."
El replies
Out of the seven rooms
Out of the eight chambers: (:35
"I know thee, my daughter, that thou art impetuous
That there is no *forbearance* among goddesses.
What dost thou wish, O Virgin Anath?"
And the Virgin Anath replies:
"Thy word, El, is wise;
Thy wisdom, unto eternity
Lucky life, thy word.
Our king is Aliyan Baal   (:40
Our ruler, there is none above him.
Let both of us drain his *chalice*
Both of us drain his *cup!*"
Loudly cries Thor-El, her father,
El, the king who brought her into being:
There cry Asherah and her sons,   (:45
The goddess and the band of her brood:
"Lo Baal has no house like the gods
Nor a court like the sons of Asherah:
The dwelling of El
The shelter of his sons
The dwelling of Lady Asherah of the Sea
The dwelling of [Pidr]ay, girl of light,
[The shelter] of Ṭallay, [girl] of rain,
The dwelling [of Arṣay, girl of Yᶜbdr].
[   ]   (:VI:1
[   ] thy [h]ead
[   ] 'twixt your eyes
[   ] a thousand
[   ] a myriad   (:5
[   ] in the rivers
Cross Byblos
Cross Qᶜl
Cross Iht
Soul of blemish!
Proceed, O fisherman of Asherah!   (:10

Go, O Qadish-Amrar! [23]

Then shalt thou surely set face toward all glorious Ḥ(q)kpt

Caphtor is the throne on which he sits   (:15

  Ḥkpt, the land of his inheritance [24]

By the thousand acres

  Myriad of hectares!

At the feet of Kotha(r) bow and fall   (:20

  Prostrate thyself and honor him!

And say to Kothar-and-Ḥasis!

  Declare to the Skilled of Handicraft:

'The message of Ali[yan Baal]

  The w[ord of Aliy the Warrior]:

(*rest missing*)

Thy *ḥš*   (pl. ix:II:1

  Thy tree(s)

    Thy *ᶜbṣ*

Let thy feet [run t]o me

  [To me let] thy legs [hast]en!

[   ] – – – and set

[   ]

[l]apis lazuli   (:5

[   ] lift, in the midst

[   ] prisoner

[   ] O Mot

[   ] like a gust

[   ] prepare for the earth   (:10

[   ] – – – prepare

[   ] pass

[   ] thy god. The court [   ]

[23] Qadish-Amrar is the pair of Asherah's messengers fused into one entity. Double names of deities are exceedingly common in the ancient Near East, e.g., Yahweh-Elohim in the Bible, and Amon-Re in Egypt. The notion that Yahweh-Elohim results from fusing two documents (a "J" document with Jehovah/Yahweh, and an "E" document with Elohim) completely misses the mark.

[24] This statement ties in with the fact that the main thrust of the Minoans came to Crete from Egypt. Ugaritic literature reflects a time when the hub of its culture was Caphtor (Crete), for that is where the Ugaritic god of arts and crafts is enthroned. However, his original home or "land of his inheritance" is Ḥkpt, the source of Greek *Aigyptos*, "Egypt" (from Egyptian *Ḥt-k₃-ptḥ* with the final *-ḥ* lost in accordance with Minoan phonetics, as we have noted above).

[they reach] Inbb   (:15
By the thousand [acres]
    [Myriad hectares]
[At the fe]et of Anath [they bow and fall]
    [Prostrate] themselves and [honor her]
[They lift their voices]
    [And] shout:
"The message [of Thor-El, thy father]
    [The word of L]ṭpn, thy begetter:
'[Put bre]ad [in the earth]
    Set [mandrakes] in the du[st]   (:20
[Pour a peace offering] into the midst of the earth
    [A libation into the midst of the] fields.
Thy ḥš
    [Thy tree(s)]
        [Thy ᶜbṣ].
[To me] let thy [fe]et run.' "
[Thereupon she sets face] toward the mountain
[   ] – – number
[   ]   (:25
[Caphtor] is throne [whereon he sits]:   (:III:1
    [Ḥkpt, the land of his inheritance].
By the thousand acres
    My[riad of hectares].
"[At the feet of Kothar] bow and fall
    [Prostrate yourselves and honor him]!
And say to Koth[ar-and-Ḥasis]!
    [Declare to the Skilled of Handic]raft: (:5
'[The message of Thor-El, thy father]
    The word of Lṭpn, [thy begetter],
– – – Kothar [   ]
place – – – – – [   ]
put – – – – – [   ]
Thy ḥš   (:10
    Thy tree(s)
        Thy ᶜbṣ.
[Let thy feet run to me]
    To me let [thy] le[gs] hasten!
[   ] the mountain of the cup.

For [I have a w]ord that I shall tell thee
    A matter that I shall declare to thee
'Tis the word of the tree
    And the whisper of the stone
       The murmur of the heavens to [the earth]
        [Of the deep to the stars].
A word that men do not know   (:15
    [Nor the multitudes of the earth understand].
Come and I shall show [it]
In the midst of the mountain of me, god of Saphon.' "
And Kothar-and-Ḥasis replies:
"Ye are slow
    But I [am fast]!
[Caphtor] is not distant, O gods!
    Ḥkp[t is not distant, O deities]!
Two *stages* under [the springs of the earth]   (:20
    Three *marches* (aloft in)] the *hills*."
Then he set[s face toward Ltpn], God of Mercy,
In the midst of the mountai[n   ]
He enters the abode of E[l]
    [And comes into the domicile of the king], Father of Šnm.
At [the feet of El he bows and falls]
    Prostrates himself [and honors him].   (:25
Thor-El [   ]
hurry [   ]
thy house [   ]
build [   ]
(*two lines missing*)
Aloud he cries to wa[ke the gods   ]   (pl. x:IV:2
are not distant, O [   ]
called El, sits in [his festival house   ]
– – – – – – – – – – [   ]   (:5
gods, house of thy lord [   ]
that they do not go hurrying [   ]
in the dust, destruction – – – [   ]
give water – – – – – – – – –
He puts [a cup in the hand]
    A goblet in both hand(s). [ ]   (:10
Like Night – – – – – – [   ]

– – – – – – his son(s), Thor [   ]
And Ltpn, God of Mercy, replies: [   ]
"The name of my son is Yw-El [25] [   ]."
And he proclaims the name of *Sea* [   ].   (:15
They reply: "– – – [   ]
Thou art named 'Lord' [   ]
I am Ltpn, God [of Mercy,   ]
On the hands, thou art named [   ]
Thy name is El's Darling, [Sea   ]   (:20
My house of silver which [   ]
In the hands of Aliyan Ba[al   ]
A pitcher of wine – – – [   ]
Drive him out from the se[at of his kingship]
   [From the dais, the throne,] of his sovereignty   (:25
[   ]
And they, even to [   ]
He will smite thee like [   ]
El, sacrifice [   ]
to name [   ]
Slaughter great [and small cattle]   (:30
   [Kill] oxen and [fatlings of rams]
      [Yearling bullocks]
         [Little] lambs, [kids   ]
(two or three lines missing)   (:V:1
[   ] soul [   ]
[Ha]dd approaches him
[   ] in Saphon   (:5
[   ] blowing, in answering/seeing
[   ] weeping he answers/sees
         surely] did [not] know
[   ]tie
[   ] bind   (:10
[   ] the builder of stones – – – –
[   ] and the mountain of my loins

[25] "Yw-El" is the son of the head of the pantheon. This suggests that
"Yahweh" ("Yw") was originally El's son in pre-Israelite Canaan. It is usual
for a younger god to eclipse the older gods in the development of religion.
In other words, just as Zeus eclipsed his father Cronus, Yahweh eclipsed his
father El. Subsequently, Hebrew monotheism necessitated the identification
of Yahweh with El.

```
[                    ] – – – –
[                    ] – – – – – – his loins
[                    ] and a day, two days                          (:15
[                    ] arrives, the soul
[                    ] Hadd meets him
[            ] – – of thee, in Saphon
[            ] – – – – hind(s)
[            ] weeping he answers/sees                              (:20
[            ] surely did not know
[            ] bind Thor-El
[                ] tie the builder of stones
[            ] – – – – enter
[            ] my loins I – – –                                     (:25
[            ] enter – – –
[                    ] – – –
[            ] to the earth.
```

Text 51, column I, repeats that all the gods except Baal have houses. Then Kothar-and-Ḫasis, who is to build Baal's house, is described as working at his forge, smelting gold and silver to make glorious artistic creations. Column II goes on to tell how Baal and Anath enlisted Asherah's help in securing permission for Baal to get his palace. Column III describes Baal expressing to the assemblage of the gods his chagrin at past humiliations. After Asherah reminds Baal and Anath that they must get El's permission for the palace, the gods settle down to a banquet. Columns IV and V narrate how Asherah journeys to El's abode and cajoles him into authorizing the construction of the palace from gold, silver, and lapis lazuli. Anath conveys the good news to Baal. Then Kothar-and-Ḫasis is summoned, and after eating and drinking, he discusses the specifications of the house with Baal.

Columns V–VI record the disagreement between Kothar-and-Ḫasis, who advocates a window, and Baal who refuses to have it installed.[26] Kothar confidently predicts that Baal will come round to wanting the window. Meanwhile Kothar builds the palace with cedars of Lebanon

---

[26] The excavations at Ugarit convey the impression that windows were not in general use. Minoan architecture, on the other hand, included windows. The disagreement between Baal and Kothar thus reflects the introduction of windowed palaces from Crete to Ugarit.

and by applying his divine fire to the structure, converts it into a palace of gold and silver. Overjoyed, Baal gives a feast as a housewarming. Column VII refers to Baal's conquest of ninety cities and to his change of mind, as he decides to have a window installed after all. No sooner is it done than Baal is menaced by enemies and Mot claims Baal's kingship. Column VIII relates how Baal sends his pair of messengers, Gupan and Ugar, to Mot telling him that the house has been completed and (belatedly?) inviting him to a party there.

(opening lines broken) (51:I:1

"(There are) the dwelling of El
   The shelter of his sons

The dwelling of Lady Asherah of the Sea (:15
   The dwelling of the renowned brides

The dwelling of Pidray, girl of light,
   The shelter of Ṭallay, girl of rain,
      The dwelling of Arṣay, girl of Yᶜbdr.

Also something else I'll tell thee (:20
Go to!

Beseech Lady Asherah of the Sea
   Entreat the Creatress of Gods!"

The Skilled One goes up to the bellows
   In the hands of Ḥasis are the tongs. (:25

He pours silver
   He casts gold

He pours silver by thousands (of shekels)
   Gold he pours by myriads

He pours *ḥym* and *tbtḥ* (:30

A glorious *crown* weighing two myriads
   A glorious *crown* studded with silver
      Adorned with red gold.

A glorious throne
   A dais above a glorious footstool (:35
      Which *glisters* in purity.

Glorious shoes of reception
   Thereover he brings them gold.[27]

A glorious table that is full

---

[27] I.e., he covers them with gold to make gilded slippers?

Whatever – – – – of the earth's foundations.   (:40
   A glorious bowl, fine work of *Kamares*
      Set like the realm of Yman
         In which there are buffaloes by myriads.

[   ]   (51:II:1
[   ] stone [   ]
She takes hold of her spindle [   ]
   The spindle of *utility* in – – [   ]
He *adorns* her with the covering of her flesh   (:5
   She tears her clothing
On the second day
   He *adorns* her in the two rivers.
She sets a *pot* on the fire
   A *vessel* on top of the coals.
She propitiates Thor, God of Mercy,   (:10
   Entreats the Creator of Creatures.
On lifting her eyes
   She sees
Asherah sees Baal's going
   Yea the going of the Virgin Anath   (:15
      The tread of the Progenitress [of Heroes].
On it the feet [stamp]
   [On the p]lain [she breaks her] back
[Above], her [f]ace s[weats]
   The [joint]s of her [ba]ck fail
      [Her] vertebrae are agitated.   (:20
She lifts her voice
   And shouts:
"Why has Aliyan Baal come?
   Why came the Virgin Anath?
Is it that my smiters or the smiters of my sons   (:25
   [the b]and of my kin [   ]?"
[Ashe]rah sees the silver
   The shadow of silver
      And the [gleam] of gold.
Lady Asherah of the Sea is glad,
Aloud to her lad [she cries]:

"I shall entice the eye of the Skilled One.
Fisherman of Lady Asherah [of the Sea]!   (:30
Take a net in thy hand
    [The   ] of the Lady on the hands
[   ] from El's Darling
    From the sea of El [   ]
The conception of El [   ]   (:35
Aliyan [Baal   ]
    The Virgin [Anath   ]
(*about fourteen lines missing*)
[   ] let him not *tempt*   (51:III:5
[   ] to found thee
[   ] and forever
[   ] – – – – – –
[   ] O god(s) of king(ship)
[   ] Aliyan Baal   (:10
    [   ] the Rider of Clouds
[   ] he goes and reviles
    He proceeds to spit in the midst of the assembly of the gods:
"I have drunk [disgrace] from my table   (:15
    Scorn from a cup did I drink.
Baal hates two sacrifices
    Three, the Rider of Clouds:
The sacrifice of shame
    And the sacrifice of baseness
      And the sacrifice of the abuse of handmaids   (:20
For therein shame is *seen*
    And therein is the abuse of handmaids."
After Aliyan Baal came
    (And) came the Virgin Anath,
They besought Lady Asherah of the Sea   (:25
    Yea entreated the Creatress of the Gods.
And Lady Asherah of the Sea replied:
"How can ye beseech Lady Asherah of the Sea
    Yea entreat the Creatress of the Gods?   (:30
Have ye besought Thor, God of Mercy,
    Or entreated the Creator of Creatures?"
And the Virgin Anath replied:
"We do beseech Lady Asherah of the Sea

We entreat the Creatress of Gods.   (:35
[   ] we beseech him
[   ] Aliyan Baal
[   ] Lady Asherah of the Sea
[   ] the Virgin Anath
[The gods] eat (and) drink   (:40
  And those that suck [the breast qua]ff,[28]
[With a ke]en [knife
  A slice] of fatling.
[They drink] wine from a goblet
  [From a cup of gold, the bl]ood of vines,
(*nine lines broken*)
Thor-[El   Lady]   (51:IV:1
Asherah [of the Sea]
And [   ] Lady
Asherah of the Sea [declares]:
"[Saddle an ass],
  Hitch a donkey!   (:5
Put [on harness of] silver
  [Trappings] of gold
    Prepare the harness of my jennies!"
Qadish-and-Amrar hearkens
He saddles an ass

[28] The reading is certain from duplicated passages. On an ivory panel from the royal bedstead in the Ugaritic palace, the sucklings are represented as a pair of kings sucking the breasts of a goddess (*Antiquity*, 29, 1955, plate VII). The idea of kings receiving their greater-than-life-size status by being nursed by a goddess was widespread in Mesopotamia and especially in Egypt. What is interesting at Ugarit is the duality of the royal sucklings. I suggest, with all due reserve, that this may reflect dyarchy at Ugarit (with two kings reigning simultaneously, as at Sparta). This would also explain the letter (*PRU IV*, p. 111) to Niqmepa from Niqmad, in which the latter addresses Niqmepa as his "brother," without royal titles. Since the letter was found in the palace, Niqmepa must have been the king of that name. And since neither name is accompanied by royal titles, the two correspondents must have been equals. If (as Nougayrol suggests) Niqmad was presumably king of some other realm, we should expect Niqmepa to be called "king of Ugarit" and Niqmad to be called the king of whatever country he ruled. Dyarchy is the simplest explanation. It is also interesting to note that the text in *PRU IV*, p. 141, is sealed by two Amorite kings: Aziru, king of Amurru, and Shaushgamuwa, king of Amurru. While it is always possible that one of the seals belonged to a former king, the two seals may indicate dyarchy in the kingdom of Amurru too. Dyarchy was common in the ancient East Mediterranean; it is thus attested among the Spartans, Lycians, Midianites, and others.

Hitches a donkey
Puts a harness of silver   (:10
 Trappings of gold
  Prepares the harness of her jennies.
Qadish-and-Amrar embraces
 He sets Asherah on the back of the ass
  On the beautiful back of the donkey. (:15
Qadish begins to light the way
 Even Amrar like a star.
Forward goes the Virgin Anath
 And Baal departs for the heights of Saphon.
Then she sets face toward El   (:20
At the sources of the Two Rivers
 In the midst of the streams of the Two Deeps.
She enters the abode of El
 And comes into the domicile of the King, Father of Šnm. (:25
At the feet of El she bows and falls
 Prostrates herself and honors him.
As soon as El sees her
 He cracks a smile and laughs.
His feet he sets on the footstool
 And twiddles his fingers   (:30
He lifts his voice
 And shouts:
"Why has Lady Asherah of the Sea come
 Why came the Creatress of Gods?
Art thou hungry?
 Then have [a morsel]!
Or art thou thirsty?
 Then have [a drink]!
Eat!   (:35
 Or drink!
Eat bread from the tables!
 Drink wine from the goblets!
  From a cup of gold, the blood of vines!
If the love of El moves thee
 Yea the affection of Thor arouses thee!"
And Lady Asherah of the Sea replies: (:40
"Thy word, El, is wise;

Thou art wise unto eternity;
 Lucky life is thy word.
Our King is Aliyan Baal
 Our judge, and none is above him.
Let both of us drain his *chalice*   (:45
 Both of us drain his cup!"
Loudly Thor-El, her father, shouts,
 King El who brought her into being;
There shout Asherah and her sons
 The goddess and the band of her brood: (:50
"Lo there is no house unto Baal like the gods
 Nor a court like the sons of Asherah:
The dwelling of El
 The shelter of his sons
The dwelling of Lady Asherah of the Sea
 The dwelling of the renowned brides.
The dwelling of Pidray, girl of light,   (:55
 The shelter of Ṭallay, girl of rain,
  The dwelling of Arṣay, girl of Yᶜbdr."
And Lṭpn, God of Mercy, replied:
"Am I to act as a lackey of Asherah
 And am I to act like the holder of a trowel? (:60
If the handmaid of Asherah will make the bricks
A house shall be built for Baal like the gods (:V:63
 Yea a court like the sons of Asherah."
And Lady Asherah of the Sea replied:
"Thou are great, O El,   (:65
Thou art verily wise!
 The gray of thy beard hath verily instructed thee!
(Here are) *pectorals* of [ ] for thy breast.
Lo, also it is the time of his rain.
Baal sets the season – – – – – – –
And gives forth his voice from the clouds   (:70
 He flashes lightning to the earth.
As a house of cedars let him complete it
 Or a house of bricks let him erect it!
Let it be told to Aliyan Baal:
'Call the – – – – into thy house   (:75
 The – – – – – in the midst of thy palace!

The mountains will bring thee much silver
 The hills, the choicest of gold;
   The mines will bring thee precious stones
And build a house of silver and gold   (:80
 A house of lapis gems!' "
The Virgin Anath rejoices.
She jumps with the feet
 And leaves the earth.
Then she sets face toward the Lord of Saphon's crest   (:85
By the thousand acres
 Yea myriad hectares.
The Virgin Anath laughs.
She lifts her voice
 And shouts:
"Be informed, Baal!
 Thy news I bring!
A house shall be built for thee as for thy brothers   (:90
 Even as court as for thy kin.
Call the – – – – – into thy house
 The – – – – – in the midst of thy palace.
The mountains will bring thee much silver
 The hills the choicest of gold   (:95
And build a house of silver and gold
 A house of lapis gems!"
Aliyan Baal rejoices.
He calls the – – – – – into his house
 The – – – – – in the midst of his palace.
The mountains bring him much silver   (:100
 The hills, the choicest of gold;
   The mines bring him precious stones.
Kothar-and-Ḥasis is sent.

And return to the story: when the lads are sent [29]   (:105

After Kothar-and-Ḥasis arrived
He sets an ox in front of him

---

[29] These words are a notation of the scribe, not part of the story. Apparently there was a pause in the copying or dictation of the poem, and this note tells the scribe or narrator where to continue at the next sitting.

A fatling directly before him.
A chair is placed
   And he is seated
      At the right of Aliyan Baal   (:110
Until they have eaten
   (And) drunk.
And Aliya[n Baal] declares:
"[   ]
[Hur]ry, let a house [be built]
   Hurry, let a pal[ace] be erected!
Hurry, let a house be built   (:115
   Hurry, let a palace be erected!
      In the midst of the heights of Saphon!
A thousand acres the house is to comprise
   A myriad hectares, the palace!"
And Kothar-and-Ḫasis declares: (:120
"Hear, O Aliyan Baal!
   Perceive, O Rider of Clouds!
I shall surely put a window in the house
   A casement in the midst of the palace!"
And Aliyan Baal replies: (:125
"Do not put a window in the ho[use]
   A [case]ment in the midst of the palace!"
(rest of column missing)
And Kothar-and-Ḫasis replies: (51:VI:1
"Thou wilt return, Baal, to [my word]."
Again Kothar-and-Ḫasis spoke:
"Hear, O Aliyan Baal!
I shall surely put a window in the house   (:5
   A casement in the midst of the palace!"
And Aliyan Baal replies:
"Do not put a window in the house
   A casement in the midst of the palace!
Let not [Pidr]ay, girl of light,   (:10
   [Nor Ṭall]ay, girl of rain,
[   ] El's [bel]oved Sea [   ]"
[   ] he reviles and spits [   ].
And Kothar-and-Ḫasis replies: (:15
"Thou wilt return, Baal, to my word."

[Of cedars] his house is to be built
  [Of bricks] is his palace to be erected.
He [goe]s to Lebanon and its trees
  To Syria (and) the choicest of its cedars.
L[o], Lebanon and its trees   (:20
  Syria (and) the choicest of its cedars.
Fire is set on the house
  Flame on the palace.
Behold a day and a second
  The fire eats into the house   (:25
    The flame into the palace.
A third, a fourth day
  The fire eats into the house
    The flame into the palace.
A fifth, a sixth day
  The fire eats into the house   (:30
    The flame [in the midst of the pala]ce.
Behold on the seve[nth] d[ay]
  The fire departs from the house
    The flame from the palace.
Silver turns from blocks
  Gold is turned from bricks.   (:35
Aliyan Baal rejoices.
"My house have I built of silver
  My palace of gold have I made."
[His] house, [Baa]l prepares
  Hadd prepares the [housewarm]ing of his palace.   (:40
He slaughters great [and] small cattle
  He fells oxen [and] ram-fatlings
Yearling calves
  Little lambs (and) kids.
He called his brothers into his house
  His kinsmen into the midst of this palace   (:45
    He called the seventy sons of Asherah.
He caused the sheep gods to drink wi[ne].
  He caused the ewe goddesses to drink [wine].
He caused the bull gods to drink w[ine]
  He caused the cow goddesses to drink [wine].   (:50
He caused the throne gods to drink wine

He caused the chair goddesses to drink [wine].
He caused the jar gods to drink wine
   He caused the jug goddesses to drink [wine].
Until the gods had eaten and drunk   (:55
   And the sucklings quaffed
With a keen knife
   A slice of fatling.
They drink [win]e from a goblet
   [From a cup of gold, the blood of vines].
(*five lines missing*)
[lapis] lazul[i   ]   (51:VII:1
[   ] Aliyan Baal
[   ] El's Darling, Se[a],
[   ] on top of his head
El [*lau*]*ghed* in the mountain   (:5
Like [ ] gods in Saphon
– – – to [   ] towns
   Return to [ ] cities
He took sixty-six towns
   Yea seventy-seven cities   (:10
Eighty, Baal [   ]
   Ninety, Baal [   ]
As Baal [went] into the midst of the house
Aliyan Baal declared: (:15
"I would install, Kothar, son of the Sea,
   Yea Kothar, son of the Assembly!
Let a casement be opened in the house
   A window in the midst of the palace
And let the clouds be opened with rain
   On the op[ening] of Kothar-and-Ḥasis."
Kothar-and-Ḥasis laughed.
He lifts his voice
   And shouts:
"Did I not tell thee, O Aliyan Baal,
   That thou wouldst return, Baal, to my word: (:25
'Let a casement be opened in the house
   A window in the midst of the palace!'"
Baal [op]ened the [cloud]s with rain
His holy voice he gives forth in [the heavens]

Again Baal [   ] his [   ]   (:30
His h[oly] voice [   ] earth
[   ] mountains. I shall invade
[   ]
the easterners; the back [ ] they jump.   (:35
The enemies of Baal seize the forests
  The foes of Hadd, the fringes of the mountain.
And Aliyan Baal declares:
"Enemies of Hadd, why do ye invade
  Why do ye invade the *arsenal of our defense?*"
Baal's eyes are before his hands   (:40
  (Witnessing) that they *wrest* the cedar from his right hand.
Weeping, Baal returns to his house:
"Whether King
  Or Commoner
Be *invested* with sovereignty (over) the land
Respects I shall not send to the god Mot   (:45
  Nor *greetings* to El's Beloved, the Hero!"
Mot calls from his throat
  The Beloved meditates in his inwards:
"I alone am he who will rule over the gods   (:50
  Yea command gods and men
    Even domin[ate] the multitudes of the earth."
Aloud Baal cries to his l[ad]s:
"Look, [Gupan] and Ugar, son(s) of Ġalmat,
  Errand lad(s), son(s) of Ẓalmat
    The lo[fty] (and) [distinguished]!
[   ] scorched; a flock [   ] clouds
[under   ]
(*two lines broken*)
Then surely set face   (51:VIII:1
Toward the mountain of Trġzz
  Toward the mountain of Ṭrmg
    Toward the furrow of the *thriving* of the earth.
Lift the mountain on the hands   (:5
  The hill on top of the palms
And go down into the nether-reaches of the earth
  So that you will be counted among those who go down into the
        earth!   (:10

Then shall ye set face
Toward his city, Hmry.
Lo the throne on which he sits
  – – – the land of his inheritance
   And the guards of the defense of the gods.   (:15
Do not draw near the god Mot
Lest he make you like a lamb in his mouth
  Like a kid in his jaws ye be crushed!   (:20
The Luminary of the Gods, Sun, burns
  The heavens halt on account of El's Darling, Mot.
By the thousand acres   (:25
  Yea myriad hectares
At the feet of Mot bow and fall
  Prostrate yourselves and honor him!
And say to the god Mot   (:30
  Declare to El's beloved, the Hero:
'The message of Aliyan Baal
  The [wor]d of Aliy the W[arrior]:   (:35
"My house I have built [of silver]
  [My palace of gold   ]
[   ] my brother(s)
[   ] my brother(s)
(*two lines broken*)   (:40
[   ] I invited
[   ]
[   ] gods
[   ] love/hand
[   ] *thee*." ' "
[Gupan]-and-Ugar.

[   ] the T^c-ite; Niqmad, king of Ugarit.[30] (:edge
"How can they beseech Lady Asherah [of the Sea] (frag. for restoring
                VII:53–58

 Even entreat the Creatress of the Gods
That a house be given to Baal like the gods

  [30] This line, on the edge of the tablet, is a colophon giving the name of the
scribe (who belonged to the influential tribe of Tha^c) and the name of the
king (Niqmad II) during whose reign the tablet was written.

Even a court like the sons of Asherah?"   (:5
Aloud Baal shouts to his lads:
"Look, Gupan and Ugar, sons of Ġalmat,
  Errand lads, sons of Ẓalmat
    The lofty, (and) distinguished!
[   ] scorched, a flock   (:10
clouds under [   ]
birds [   ]
– – – – – – [   ]
– – *lightning* [   ]
O Mot/die [   ]   (:15
As[ked   ]

Text 67 opens with the statement that because Baal smote Leviathan, Mot intends to devour Baal (thus inaugurating a seven-year cycle of dearth). Column II tells of Baal's capitulation to Mot. Column III, which is fragmentary, seems to refer to what will happen to the fertility of the flocks. Column IV describes Baal at a divine banquet. Column V tells how Baal, before descending into the underworld of Mot, impregnates a heifer who bears him a son. Column VI narrates how El, on hearing of Baal's death, goes into mourning. Meanwhile Anath searches for Baal's corpse and at last finds it: the prelude to his resurrection and the re-inauguration of fertility.

"Because thou didst smite Lotan,[31] the evil serpent   (67:I:1
  Didst destroy the crooked serpent
    The mighty one of seven heads [32]
The heavens – – – – – – – – –   (:5
I shall eat – – – – – – – so that I die.
I am indeed to do down into the throat of the god Mot
  Yea into the gullet of El's Beloved, the Hero!"
The gods depart and do not sit
Then they set face toward Baal of Saphon's crest   (:10
And Gupan and Ugar say:
"The message of the god Mot

[31] "Lotan" is the Ugaritic form of the evil dragon that appears in the Bible as "Leviathan."
[32] Psalm 74:14 attributes the destruction of the many-headed Leviathan to God. The Greek myth of Heracles, who slew the seven-headed Hydra, is a reverberation of the same theme: the victory of Good over Evil.

The word of the dearest of El's sons, the Hero:

'Prepare him a sheep (for) the soul of the Lioness of Chaos   (:15

   Or (for) the appetite of the dolphin in the sea

Or the *pools* that the buffaloes *crave*

   Yea the spring of the *craving* of the hinds

Or forsooth, forsooth, the soul

   – – – – – – ass [es   ]

With both my hands I shall eat them   (:20

   My seven portions from the bowl

      Or the cup that *River* mixes.

Baal called to my brothers

   Yea Hadd invited my kin.

So eat bread with my brothers

   And drink wine with my kin.   (:25

And *I* shall place Baal

   (And) surely load (him) on thee.

Because thou didst smite [Lotan, the evi]l [serpent]

   Didst destroy [the crooked serpent]

      The mighty one [of seven heads]   (:30

[The heavens – – – – – –]' "

(*about thirty lines missing*)

[A lip to ea]rth   (67:II:1

   A lip to heaven

      [And to]ngue to the stars

So that [Baa]l may enter his inwards

   Yea descend into his mouth

As scorched is the olive   (:5

   The produce of the earth

      And the fruit of the trees." [33]

Aliyan Baal fears him

   The Rider of Clouds [34] dreads him.

"Depart! Speak to the god Mot

   Declare to El's Beloved, the Hero:

'The message of Aliyan Baal   (:10

---

[33] Vegetation will languish when Baal is swallowed by Mot.

[34] The epithet "Rider of Clouds," applied to Baal at Ugarit, was applied to Yahweh in Israel (Psalm 68:5; 68:4 in the King James Bible). The epithet is appropriate to the storm god. Hebrew monotheism necessitated the transfer of the functions of the nature gods to Yahweh, who, among other things, is god of the storm.

The word of Aliy the Warrior:
"Hail, O god Mot!
Thy slave am I
  Yea thine forever." ' "
The gods depart and do not sit.
Then they set face toward the god Mot
  Toward his city, Hmry,   (:15
Behold it is the throne of his sitting
  Yea the land of his inheritance!
They lift their voices
  And shout:
"The message of Aliyan Baal
  The word of Aliy the Warrior!
'Hail, O god Mot!
Thy slave am I
  Yea thine forever!' "   (:20
The god Mot is glad.
[He lifts] his [voice]
  And shouts:
"How can he govern
[   ] Hadd
[   ] my battle
(*about twenty-five lines missing*)
[Gre]at is the sitting [   ]   (67:III:1
  Great is the sitting [   ]
[   ] land of Ḫšn [   ]
shall – – – – – shall destroy [   ]   (:5
the brick[s] will be [   ]
of thy brickwork [   ]
compound like star[s   ]
Moreover Mot I shall call [   ]
  The Beloved from the mid[st   ]   (:10
Shall I not put [in   ]
I shall upset thee [   ]
– – – and go [   ]
And go, O gods [   ]
The pleasantest of the gods [   ]   (:15
The increase of abundan[ce of flocks   ]
The increase of abundan[ce of flocks   ]

Moreover Mot I shall cal[l   ]
The Beloved from the midst [   ]
And go, O gods [   ]   (:20
And speak to [   ]
With abundance of floc[ks   ]
  Abundance of flocks [   ]
– – – – – – [   ]
Moreover, Mot will I ca[ll   ]   (:25
  The Beloved from the mids[t   ]
– – – and go [   ]
[   ] go [   ]
(*two lines broken*)
[   ]   (67:IV:1
And for seeking [   ]
A hundred – – [   ]
[   ] seek [   ]
He lifts his voice   (:5
  [And shouts:]
"O face of Baa[l   ]
  O Hadd [   ]
Baa[l] – – – [in seven   ]
  In eight [   ]
He draws near [   ]   (:10
Bread [   ]
Until [the gods] have eaten [and drunk]
  And those who su[ck the breast] have quaffed
With a [keen] knife
  [A slice of fatling].
They drink [wine from] a gob[let]   (:15
  From a cup of go[ld, the blood of vines].
A cup of silver [   ]
  A goblet [   ]
And they piss [   ]
[Then] they go up, they [   ]   (:20
The house of El [   ]
Upon Ḥbš [   ]
Who has sent [   ]
  Sent [   ]
(*about twelve lines broken*)

[   ] Aliyan   (67:V:1
[Baal   ] – – – – –
[   ] soul of a calf [   ]   (:5
I shall put him in the grave of the gods of the earth.
And thou, take thy clouds
   Thy wind, thy storm, thy rains!
With thee thy seven lads
   Thine eight swine
With thee, Pidray, girl of light,   (:10
   With thee, Ṭallay, girl of rain.
Then thy face shalt thou set toward the mountain of Knkny.
Lift the mountain on the hands
   The hill on top of the palms
And go down to the nether-reaches of the earth   (:15
   So that thou mayest be counted among those who go down into the earth
      And Ill may know that thou art dead!"
Aliyan Baal hearkens.
He loves a heifer in Dbr
   A young cow in the fields of Šḥlmmt
He lies with her seventy-seven times   (:20
   [Yea   ] eighty-eight times
So that [she concei]ves
   And bears Mṯ.[35]
– – [   ] clad him
[   ] for him, intercede   (:25
[   ] for her bosom
(*about thirty-five lines missing*)
We came to the goodness of the land of Dbr   (67:VI:5
   To the beauty of the fields of Šḥlmmt
We came upon Baal prostrate on the earth.
Dead is Aliyan Baal
   Perished is the Prince, Lord of Earth!   (:10
Thereupon Lṭpn, God of Mercy,
   Goes down from the throne
     Sits on the footstool
       And from the footstool sits on the earth.
He pours the ashes of grief on his head   (:15

[35] The consonants of Ugaritic *Mṯ* correspond to those of Hebrew *Moshe*, "Moses."

The dust of wallowing on his pate
  For clothing, he is covered with a doubled cloak.
He roams the mountain in *mourning*
  Yea through the forest *in grief*
He cuts cheek and chin
  He lacerates his forearms   (:20
He plows (his) chest like a garden
  Like a vale he lacerates (his) back.
He lifts his voice
  And shouts:
"Baal is dead!
Woe to the people of Dagon's Son
  Woe to the multitudes of Athar-Baal!
I shall go down into the earth."   (:25
Also Anath goes
  And treads every mountain to the midst of the earth
    Every hill to the midst of the fields.
She comes to the good[ness of the land] of Dbr
  The beauty of the fields of [Šḥl]mmt   (:30
She [comes] upon Baal prostra[te on the ea]rth.
  [For clothing] she is covered with a doubl[ed cloak].

Text 62 joins onto text 49, supplying the opening part of column I
on the obverse, and the end of column VI on the reverse. Column I opens
with the title "Pertaining to Baal," implying that the ancients called this
Cycle simply *Baal*. After the title the text goes on to describe Anath's
mourning for Baal. She asks the sun goddess, Shapsh, to set Baal's corpse
on her (Anath's) shoulders. Shapsh obliges, and Anath raises the corpse
up to heights of Saphon, where she sacrifices seventy each of a whole series
of animals as a memorial offering to Baal. Then she reports the death of
Baal to El and Asherah, and requests that they appoint one of their sons as
king in Baal's place. They choose Athtar, who proves to be incapable of
ruling Saphon but makes a try at ruling the earth. Column II relates how
Anath lays hands on Mot and orders him to restore her brother. Mot
refuses but goes on to describe how he devoured Baal. The sun and other
heavenly bodies stand still in their courses for months, until Anath finds
the opportunity of destroying Mot and planting his remains in the field.
This revenge is the prelude to Baal's revival in column III. El is apprised
of Baal's return to life by a dream in which the heavens rain oil and the

wadies run with honey. Column IV tells of the search for Baal by Anath and Shapsh, the sun goddess. In column V Baal vanquishes Mot and recovers his throne. Seven years later, Mot returns to accuse Baal and challenge him to a fight. Column VI describes the fight, which ends in a tie, whereupon Shapsh arrives in time to intimidate Mot into desisting from fighting with Baal, lest El intercede and strip Mot of his throne. The text closes with references to Shapsh, El, Mot, and Kothar; to Arsh and Tannin in the sea; and to Kothar-and-Ḥasis' departure (to repair Baal's temple?). A colophon adds that Elimelech was the scribe; that the high priest Atn-Prln dictated the text; and that the tablet was written in the reign of King Niqmad.

Pertaining to Baal.   (62:obv.:1

The mountain in *mourning* she roams
   In [gr]*ief*, [through the forest]
She cuts cheek and chin
   [She lacerates] her forearms
She plows like a garden (her) chest   (:5
   Like a vale she lacerates the back.
"Baal is dead!
Woe, to the people of Dagon's son,
   Woe, to the multitudes of Athar-Baal!
Let us go down into the earth."
With her goes down the Luminary of the Gods, Sun.
Until she is sated with weeping
   She drinks tears like wine.   (:10
Aloud she cries to the Luminary of the Gods, Sun:
"Load Aliyan Baal on to me!"
The Luminary of the Gods, Sun, hearkens.
She lifts Aliyan Baal,
   On the shoulders of Anath she places him,   (:15
She raises him into the heights of Saphon
She weeps for him and buries him
   She puts him in the grave of the gods of the earth.
She sacrifices seventy buffaloes
   As an offering for Aliyan Baal.   (:20
She sacrifices seventy oxen
   [As an off]ering for Aliyan Baal.

[She sa]crifices seventy head of small cattle
   [As an of]fering for Aliyan Baal.
[She sac]rifices seventy deer
   [As an offering] for Aliyan Baal.
[She sacrifices se]venty wild goats
   [As an offering for Al]iyan Baal.   (:25
[She sacrifices seventy] asses
   [As an offering for Aliyan Baal].
(*rest of obverse missing*)
[   ] Aliyan Baal [   ]   (49:I:1
[   ] and muzzle [   ]
[   ] a brother-in-law, for the gods.
[The]n she sets face toward El   (:5
At the sources of the Two Rivers
   In the midst of the streams of the Two Deeps.
She enters the abode of El
   Goes into the domicile of the King, Father of Šnm.
At the feet of El she bends and falls
   Prostrates herself and honors him.   (:10
She lifts her voice
   And shouts:
"Let Asherah and her sons rejoice
   The goddess and the band of her brood!
For dead is Aliyan Baal,
   For perished is the Prince, Lord of Earth!"   (:15
Aloud cries El to Lady Asherah of the Sea:
"Hear, O Lady A[sherah] of the Sea!
Give one of thy so[ns] that I may make him king!"
And Lady Asherah of the Sea replies:
"Let us make king one who knows how to govern!"   (:20
And Ltpn, God of Mercy, declares:
"One feeble of *frame* will not vie with Baal
   Nor wield a spear against Dagon's son."
When the *parley is finished*
Lady Asherah of the Sea declares: (:25
"Let us make Athtar the Terrible king!
   Let Athtar the Terrible reign!"
Thereupon Athtar the Terrible
Goes into the heights of Saphon

That he may sit on the throne of Aliyan Baal.   (:30
His feet do not reach the footstool
   Nor does his head reach its top.
And Athtar the Terrible says:
"I cannot rule in the heights of Saphon!"
Athtar the Terrible goes down   (:35
   Goes down from the throne of Aliyan Baal
      That he may rule over all the grand earth.
[   ] draw from flagons
  [d]raw from jars
[   ]   (49:II:1
  And [   ]
A pitcher [   ]
  A pitcher [   ]
They pass [   ]   (:5
She approaches him
  As with the heart of a cow toward her calf
    As with the heart of a ewe toward her lamb
      So is the heart of Anath toward Baal.
She seizes Mo[t], in *ripping* (his) garment   (:10
  She closes in on [him], in tearing (his) clothes.
She lifts her voice
  And [shou]ts:
"Come, Mot, yield my brother!"
And the god Mot replies:
"What dost thou ask, O Virgin Anath?
I was going   (:15
  And roaming
Every mountain to the midst of the earth
  Every hill to the midst of the fields.
A soul was missing among men
  A soul of the multitudes of the earth.
I arrived at the goodness of the land of Dbr   (:20
  The beauty of the fields of Šḥlmmt.
I met Aliyan Baal
  I made him like a lamb in my mouth
    Like a kid in my jaws was he crushed."
The Luminary of the Gods, Sun, glows
  The heavens stop on account of the god Mot.   (:25

A day, two days pass
  From days to months.
The Maiden Anath meets him
As with the heart of a cow toward her calf
  As with the heart of a ewe toward her lamb
    So is the heart of Anath toward Baal.   (:30
She seizes the god Mot
With a sword she cleaves him
  With a pitchfork she winnows him
    With fire she burns him
      In millstones she grinds him
        In the fields she plants him
So that the birds do not eat his flesh
  Nor the fowl destroy his portion
Flesh calls to flesh.

(opening lines missing)
"For perished is [the Prince, Lord of Earth].   (49:III:1
And if A[liyan Baal] is alive
  And if the Prince, Lor[d of Earth], exists,
In a dream of Ltpn, God of Mercy,
  In a vision of the Creator of Creatures   (:5
Let the heavens rain oil
  The wadies run with honey
That I may know that Aliyan Baal is alive
  That the Prince, Lord of Earth, exists."
In a dream of Ltpn, God of Mercy   (:10
  In a vision of the Creator of Creatures
The heavens rain oil
  The wadies run with honey.
Ltpn, God of Mercy, rejoices.
His feet he sets on the footstool   (:15
  He cracks a smile and laughs.
He lifts his voice
  And shouts:
"Let me sit and rest
  And let my soul repose in my breast
For Aliyan Baal is alive   (:20

For the Prince, Lord of Earth, exists."
Aloud shouts El to the Virgin Anath:
"Hear, O Virgin Anath:
Say to the Luminary of the Gods, Sun:
'*Over the furrows* of the fields, O Sun,   (49:IV:25
    Over the furrows of the fields let El set thee.
As for the Lord of the Plowed *Furrows,*
Where is Aliyan Baal?
    Where is the Prince, Lord of Earth?' "
The Virgin Anath departs   (:30
Then she sets face toward the Luminary of the Gods, Sun.
She lifts her voice
    And shouts:
"The message of Thor-El, thy father,
    The word of Ltpn, thy begetter: (:35
'*Over the furrows* of the fields, O Sun,
    Over the furrows of the fields let El [set thee]!
As for the Lord of the *Furrows* of his plowing,
Where is Aliyan Baal?
    Where is the Prince, Lord of Earth?' "   (:40
And the Luminary of the Gods, Sun, replies:
"*Fields of wine well up* in the — — —
At night, thy kinsmen [   ]
    And I shall seek Aliyan Baal."
And the Virgin Anath answers: (:45
"(As for) me, 'tis not I, O Sun!
    (As for) me, 'tis not I, (but) El summo[ns thee]
May [   ] guard thee [   ]"
(*eight lines broken*)
Baal seizes the son of Asherah   (49:V:1
    The great *one* he smites on the shoulder
        The *tyrant* he smites with a stick.
Mot is vanquished
    Reaches earth.
[*Baal returns*] to the throne of his kingship   (:5
    [*Dagon's son*] to the seat of his sovereignty
From [days] to months
    From months to years
        [Lo] in the seventh year

And the god Mot [*addresses himself*] to Aliyan Baal.   (:10
He lifts his voice
   And shouts:
"Because of thee, O Baal, I have experienced humiliation
   Because of thee, experienced scattering by the sword
      Because of thee, experienced burning in fire
         Because of thee, [experienced gr]inding in the millstones   (:15
Because of thee exper[ienced   ] – – –
   Because of thee, experien[ced   ] in the fields
      Because of thee, experienced being sown in the sea. [   ]
After I shall eat and – – –   (:20
[   ]
I shall look – – [   ]
Behold [   ] I shall prosper [   ]
[   ] I shall destroy [   ]
[   ] destroy the multitud[es   ]   (:25
(*three lines broken*)
[He ex]pels him [   ]   (49:VI:1
   [He dr]ives him out [   ]
(*two lines broken*)
[   ] Mot   (:5
[   ] nations
[   ] the god Mot
[   ] his seven lads
[   ] the god Mot
And lo, (as) a brother of Sea, Baal is given   (:10
As *retribution* for the *destroyed* sons of my mother."
He returns to the Lord of the heights of Saphon,
He lifts his voice
   And shouts:
"A brother of Sea thou art made, O Baal!
As *retribution* for the *destroyed* sons of my mother!"   (:15
They *shake each other* like *gmr*-beasts
   Mot is strong, Baal is strong.
They gore like buffaloes
   Mot is strong, Baal is strong.
They bite like serpents
   Mot is strong, Baal is strong.
They kick like racing beasts

Mot is down, Baal is down.
Up comes Sun
  She cries to Mot:
"Hear, O god Mot!
How canst thou fight with Aliyan Baal?   (:25
  How will Thor-El, thy father, not hear thee?
Will he not remove the support(s) of thy throne?
  Nor upset the seat of thy kingship?
    Nor break the scepter of thy rule?"
The god Mot is afraid,   (:30
  El's Beloved, the Hero, is frightened.
Mot is roused from his prostration
[   ] Baal sets him
His kingship [   ]
  His sovereignty [   ]
[   ]
[   ] behold [   ]
[   ] years [   ]
(*six lines missing*)
[   ] thou shalt not proceed   (62:rev.:41
fresh [bread   ]
Also thou shalt not eat the [br]ead of entreaty
  Nor drink the wine of intercession.
The Sun *looks after* the deities.   (:45
  The Sun *looks after* the divinities.
Unto thee, O El, behold Mot!
  Unto thee (is) Kothar, thy companion
    Yea Ḥasis, thine acquaintance!
In the sea is Arsh and Tannin   (:50
Kothar-and-Ḥasis proceeds
Kothar-and-Ḥasis leaves.

The scribe is Elimelech, the Šbn-ite.[36]
The narrator is Atn-prln, chief of the priests (and) chief
of the herdsmen, the Tᶜ-ite.
(dated in the reign of) Niqmad, King of Ugarit,
Master of Yrgb, Lord of Ṭrmn.[37]

[36] The scribe Elimelech belonged to the Šbn tribe.
[37] Note the threefold title of King Niqmad.

Text 76 tells of Baal's departure from his palace to hunt with bow and arrow. The winged goddess Anath flies to meet Baal in the field. Then she sees a cow. Baal apparently impregnates the cow, for after a break in the tablet, Baal is described as going up to his mountain palace, where he sits upon his throne, until Anath comes to inform him that a bull calf has been born to him.

```
[                    ] the Virgin Anath                    (76:I:1
[                    ]— —  — — — —
[                    ] lest El's son(s) know
[                    ] stars
[                    ]— — — — —                            (:5
[              Al]iyan Baal
[                    ] the Rider of Clouds
[                    ] for nations
[                    ] sits/returns on/to earth
[                    ] men/die                             (:10
[                    ]— — — — — — —
[                    ] grace(s) him
[                    ] give(s)
[                    the Virgin] Anath
   [          the Progenitress] of Heroes                  (:15
      [          ] for nations
[              sits/returns] on/to earth
[                    ] to flesh
[              m]en/[d]ie
[                    ] my hands                            (:20
```
(*three lines broken*)

"[Is Baal in his house]   (76:II:1
   [El-Hadd in the mid]st of his palace?"
And the lads of Baal reply:
"Lo Baal is in his house
   El-Hadd in the midst of his palace."   (:5
His bow he takes in his hand
   Even his arc in his right hand.
Thereupon he sets his face toward the marsh of Šmk, fu[ll of buff]aloes.
The Virgin Anath lifts wing   (:10
   She lifts wing
      And leaves in flight

Toward the marsh of šmk, full [of buffaloes].
And Aliyan Baal lifts his eyes
 Yea lifts his eyes and sees
  Yea sees the Virgin Anath   (:15
   The fairest among Baal's sisters.
In her presence he proceeds to arise
 At her feet he kneels and falls
And he lifts his voice
 And shouts:
"Mayest thou live, O my sister!   (:20
 And *prospe[r]*!
The horns of thy strength, O Virgin Anath
 Let Baal anoint the horns of thy strength
  Let Baal anoint them in flight.
We have planted my foes in the earth
 In the dust, those who rise against thy brother."   (:25
And the Virgin Anath lifts her eyes
 She lifts her eyes and sees
  Yea she sees a cow.
And she proceeds in walking
 Proceeds in walking
  And proceeds in dancing
[Among] fair ones   (:30
 Among lovely ones
[ ] to Baal Anath gives [ ]
[ ] Baal whom I [   ]
[ ] Hadd who/of the partisan(s)
[ ] Aliyan Ba[al]
[The Virg]in Ana[th   ] sees   (:35
(five lines missing)
[   ] cows [   ]   (76:III:2
An ox for the Virgin Anath [   ]
 A fine cow for the Progenitress of He[roes].
And Aliyan [Baal] declares: (:5
"Why, like – – – – upon
 Like – – – which he causes to be
Baal – – – – full [   ]
 El-Hadd full [   ]
– – – – – and the Virgin Anath   (:10

And even the fairest of [Baal's] sisters."
Baal goes up into the moun[tain]
   Dagon's Son into the [   ]
Baal returns to the thro[ne of his kingship]
   Dagon's Son, on the sea[t of his sovereignty].   (:15
To the ox, falls/voice [   ]
– – – – – – [   ]
She goes and proceeds [   ]
Among the fair
   Among the lov[ely]
The cow, the cow [   ]   (:20
A bull she bears [to Baal]
   Yea a buffalo to [the Rider of Clouds].
She embraces [   ]
   She embraces [   ]
      Yea she covers him with [   ]   (:25
[   ] his/her – – and his/her – – –
[   ] – – – – of his/her youth/young – – –,
She goes up to the Mountain of Mslmt
   Into the Mountain of Power
And she goes up weeping into Arr   (:30
Into Arr and into Saphon
   Into the good (place)
      In the Mountain of Power.
She gives forth (her) voice to Baal:
"With glorious news, be infor[med, O B]aal!
   Yea, be informed, O scion of Dagon!   (:35
For a bull [is b]orn unto Baal
   Yea a buffalo to the Rider of Clouds!"
Aliyan Baal rejoices.

Text 132 gives an erotic description of Baal's mating with Anath, who
bears him offspring. The occasion is gladdened by the Kosharot.

[   ] he is *passionate* and he takes hold of [her] vagina (132:1
[she] is *passionate* and takes hold of [his] testicles
[Aliyan] Baal *makes love* by the thousand
[The Vi]rgin Anath
[embrac]ing, conceiving and there is born   (:5

[   ] the band of Kosharot
[the Vir]gin Anath
[Ali]yan Baal
[   ] reply
(*rest fragmentary*)

Text 75 tells of Baal meeting some wild, fantastic creatures in the
desert. After seven years of flourishing, Baal falls.

(*two lines broken*)   (75:I:1
[   ] of the earth
(*three lines broken*)   (:5
[   ] like the dawn
  [   ] like the east
[   ] El, our father,
The liver, like – – they devour   (:10
 – – – like – – – they bite.
El laughs in the heart
  Yea chuckles in the liver.
"Get thee out, O Tlš, handmaid of the Moon!   (:15
  Even Dmgy, handmaid of Asherah!
Take thy *ksan*
  Thy *ḥdg*
    Thy *ḥtl* [38]
And go out into Aln in the midst   (:20
  In the midst of the wilderness of Ilšiy.
– – – I shall die
dust, mighty hand/love
Ugars!   (:25
Labor!
  Bear!
The eaters will bless thee!
  Born are the devourers!
The gods proclaim their names.
On them are horns like bulls   (:30
  And humps like buffaloes
And on them is the face of Baal.[39]

[38] The triple insignia (or rather accouterments) of Tlš.
[39] Such creatures—partly bovine, partly anthropomorphic—are to be compared with the Mesopotamian "Bull of Heaven" and the Cretan Minotaur.

Baal goes and roams
    He *lives* in the corners of the desert.   (:35
Lo there arrive the eaters
    And he finds the devourers.
Baal verily covets [40]
    Dagon's Son *desires*.
Baal seeks them with his feet   (:40
    Yea El-Hadd, with his legs.

(*three lines broken*)   (75:II:1
face [   ]
Baal [   ]   (:5
    El-Hadd [   ]
come/thou [   ]
[Baal] covets [   ]
    The god *desi*[*res*   ]   (:10
[   ]
a day/Sea
[   ]
eats [   ]   (:15
like [   ]
(*six lines broken*)
Baal [   ]
    El-Hadd [   ]
Come thou indeed [   ]
B[aal] gathers them [   ]   (:25
    Dagon's Son [   ]
– – – – [   ]
latter end [   ]
did drain his cup [   ]
Mighty *idm* [   ]   (:30
    Terrible *idm* [   ]
sees/answers Baal [   ]
names him; seizes [   ]

---

[40] Baal is a coveting god. The same word appears here in Ugaritic (*hmd*) as in the Commandment "Thou shalt not covet." The biblical Commandment was evidently prompted, or at least intensified, by the Hebrew will to oppose Canaanite religion.

feet of Baal, seize [   ]
and destroy the [   ]   (:35
seize the eaters [   ]
falls in *mšmš* [   ]
In the *flanks* it is hot [   ]
  In the loins feverish [   ].
His horns like [   ]   (:40
  He, like scorching [   ]
both – – – – [   ]
– – – – – – – – [   ]
the daughters of the field, burn[ing]
Seven years the god is abundant [   ]   (:45
  Even eight cycles,[41] until [   ]
For he is clad as in the garb of [his] bro[thers]
  As with the robe of his kinsmen.
For his seventy-seven brothers ch[anced upon him]
  Yea his eighty-eight siblings found him   (:50
    And there have found him his relatives.
At the investiture of governors
  At the appointment of seasons
So fell Baal [   ] like a bull   (:55
  Yea Hadd [   ] collapsed like a buffalo
    In the midst of *mšmš*

– – – – – – – – – –
A fire – – – – – – – – [   ]
The King of Dan set thee
  The drawer at the well set thee   (:60
    The well at the house of El set thee
Yea the depth of the house of sorcery [   ].

Text 52 has to do with fertility over a seven-year (or climactically, eight-year) period, induced dramatically through invoking the precedent of El, who impregnated two women so that they bore the Seven Good Gods of fertility.

[41] "Cycle" here is a synonym for "year." This Ugaritic passage may tie in with the "eight year period" of the Minoans (*cf.* R. W. Hutchinson, *Prehistoric Crete*, pp. 236–237).

I invoke the gods go[od] and fair   (52:1
   Sons of Sharru[ma   ]
     Devotees of the city on high [   ]
in the wilderness, *hills* [   ]
to their head and [   ]   (:5
Eat of any bread!
   And drink of any liquor of wine!
Peace, O King!
   Peace, O Queen!
Choristers [42] and soldiers!

Death-and-Evil sits;
In his hand is the staff of privation
   In his hand the staff of bereavement,
They prune him with the prunings of the vine
   They switch him with the switches of the vine   (:10
     He is felled in his field like a vine.

Seven times it is recited to the accompaniment of the lute and the
choristers declaim:

And the field is the field of the gods
   The field of Asherah-and-Raḥm! [43]
By the fire, seven times the heroes
Coo[k a ki]d in milk
   A *lamb* in butter
And by the flame, seven times, the offer[ing]   (:15

Raḥmay goes and roams [   ]
   She grapples with the goodly hero [   ]
And – – – the choristers [   ]

The dwellings of the gods, eight [   ]
seven times: (:20

---

[42] Literally, "those who enter." Since the text is dramatic, they may have
formed part of the chorus.

[43] This Raḥm ("Girl," presumably referring to Anath) appears in Genesis
49:25.

I have zeal for the names
of the sons of Sharruma

I invoke the Good Gods
  [Islanders, sons of the s]ea,
    Who suck at the nipples of the breasts of Asherah [   ]
Sun *illumines* their doors [   ]   (:25
and the grapes.
Peace, O choristers, sold[iers]!
  Going with a goodly sacrifice.

The field of the gods (is) the field of Asherah-and-Raḥmay
[   ]

[   ] the shore of the sea   (:30
  And roams the shore of the deep.
[El takes] two effigies
  Two effigies from the top of the fire.
Lo she from the bottom
  Lo she rises
Lo she cries "Father, Father!"
  Lo she cries "Mother, Mother!"
"Let El's hand [44] be long like the sea
  Yea, El's hand like the flood!"
El's hand became long like the sea
  Yea, El's hand like the flood.   (:35
El takes two effigies
  Two effigies from the top of the fire.
He takes and puts (them) in his house.
El lowers his rod
  El lets down the staff of his hand.
He raises, he shoots heavenward
  He shoots a bird in the heavens
    He cleans and sets it on the coal(s).
El tests the two women.
If the women will shout:
"O husband, husband!   (:40

[44] Referring to El's *membrum virile;* this word (*yad,* "hand") sometimes
has this meaning in biblical Hebrew too.

Thy rod has fallen
     Lowered is the staff of thy hand!"——
While the bird roasts on the fire
     Broils on the coals——
The two women are wives of El
     Wives of El and his forever.
But if the women shout:
"O father, father!
Thy rod has fallen
     Lowered is the staff of thy hand!"——
While the bird roasts on the fire
     Even broils on the coals——
The two girls are daughters of El
     Daughters of El and his forever.[45]
And lo the two women shout:
"O husband, husband!
Thy rod has fallen
     Lowered is the staff of thy hand!"——
While the bird roasts on the fire
     Even broils on the coals——
So the women are wi[ves of El],
     Wives of El and his forever.
He bends
     Kis[ses] their lips
Lo their lips are sweet   (:50
     Sweet as grapes.[46]
From kissing there is conception
     From embracing there is childbirth
They go into tra[vail]
     So that they bear
Dawn
     And Dusk.
Word is brought to El:
"The wi[ves] of El have b[or]ne!

[45] Marriage, divorce, slavery, various kinds of ownership, and even adoption could be on a temporary or permanent basis. The force of this passage is that the rite will result in enduring fertility (with a virile god impregnating his permanent wives) or in enduring sterility (with an impotent god with whom the girls must remain permanently as daughters).

[46] Or "pomegranates."

What have they borne?"
"My two children
   Dawn and Dusk!
Lift up, prepare for Lady Sun
   And for the stars [   ]."
He bends, their lips he kisses   (:55
   Lo their lips are sweet.
From kissing there is conception
   [From] embracing there is childbirth
      They again [   ]
count(s) to five [   ]
the combination of the twain:
"They go into travail
And they bear
   They bear the Good [Gods]
      The Islanders, Sons of the Sea,
         Who suck from the nipples of the [Lady's] breasts!"
Word is brought to El:
"My two wives, O El, have borne! [47]
   What have they borne?"
"The Good Gods [   ]
   The Islanders, Sons of the Sea
      Who suck from the nipples of the Lady's breasts!"
A lip to earth
   A lip to heaven
But there do not enter their mouth
Birds of heaven
   And fish from the sea.[48]
And there proceed [   ]
Set(s) both right and left in their mouth.
"The wives I have wed have borne the Heptad.
O sons I have begotten!   (:65
Lift up, make preparations
In the midst of the wilderness of Kadesh!
There you would be a client

---

[47] The speaker is the human husband of the women impregnated by El. The mating of gods with women is familiar from Greek and other ancient literatures. *Cf.* Alcmene, wife of Amphitryon, who bore Heracles to Zeus.

[48] I.e., there is not enough food. The text therefore goes on to usher in a cycle of plenty.

Of the stones
  And of the trees
Seven complete years
  Yea eight cycles [49]
Until the Good Gods walk the field
  Roam the corners of the desert."
And the guard of the sown meets them.
And they call to the guard of the sown:
"O guard, guard, open!"   (:70
And he opened an aperture for them
  And they entered.
"If [there is   ] bread, give that we may eat!
  If there is [wine   ] give that we may drink!"
And the guard of the sown answered them:
"[There is bread to eat]
  There is wine to drink in [   ]"
He arrived at the *hin* [50]   (:75
  A *log* of his wine [   ]
And his companions, full of wine [   ].

Text 77 also deals with fertility, but within the framework of the moon
cult. Yariḫ, the moon god, insists on marrying Nikkal (the Mesopotamian
moon goddess), for she alone is destined to bear the right scion. Resisting
all attempts to persuade him to marry one or another prospective bride,
he insists on Nikkal's hand and pays a handsome bride-price to her family.

I sing of Nikkal-and-Ib [   ]   (77:1
Ḫrḫb, King of Summer,
  Ḫrḫb, Estival King.
When the Sun sets
  The Moon *shines*
- -
The virg[in] will give birth [51] [   ]   (:5

---

[49] The seven- (or eight-) year cycle of dearth has drawn to a close, so that
the time has come to begin a new cycle of plenty.
[50] The *hin* and *log* are measures.
[51] No virgin birth is implied here. The word *btlt*, "virgin," really means a
young woman, who may or may not be a virgin. No language in the ancient

O Kosharot
O Daughters of shouting
[The swallows]!
Lo the maid will bear a s[on   ]
answers/sees, lo for his love she is [   ]
[   ] for her flesh, my blood [   ]
And wine like/and a suitor [   ]   (:10
"Hear, O Kosharot goddesses [   ]
[   ] for his love, she is [   ]
for [her] lord [   ]
Dagon [   ]" [   ]
"[Hear], O Kosharot   (:15
[Daughters] of shout[ing]
[Swal]lows!
The Moon, illuminator of heaven, sends to Ḥr[ḫ]b, King of Summer
        (saying):
"Give Nikkal!
Moon would wed Ib
So that she may enter his house.
And I shall pay as her marriage price to her father   (:20
A thousand (shekels) of silver
A myriad of gold
I shall send e'en lapis gems.
I shall make her field into a vineyard
The field of her love into an orchard."
And Ḥrḫb, King of Summer, replies to the favorite of the gods: (:25
"O son-in-law of Baal!
Wed Pidray, gi[rl of light]!
I'll bring thee near her father, Baal.
Athtar would agree to marry off to thee Ybrdmy
The daughter of his father   (:30
The Lion [52] may be *appealed to*."
And there replies the Moon

Near East (not even Latin or Greek) has a word that necessarily means *virgo
intacta*. The Hebrew word translated "virgin" can refer even to a woman who
has been married and widowed (Joel 1:8). Whenever the Bible intends to
convey the meaning of *virgo intacta*, it adds a qualifying phrase to make the
matter clear. Genesis 24:16 therefore calls Rebecca "a virgin whom no man had
known."

[52] An epithet of Athtar.

Illuminator of Heaven
And it was answered: [53]
"With Nikkal is my wedding!"
As Moon weds Nikkal,
Her father sets the beam of the balances
    Her mother, the trays of the balances   (:35
Her brothers arrange the *ingots*
    Her sisters are for the stones of the balances.
To Nikkal-and-Ib do I sing:
"The Moon is bright
    And may the Moon shed light on thee."

I sing of the Kosharot goddesses   (:40
    Daughters of shouting
        Swallows
            Daughters of the New Moon
                Lord of the Sickle.
Going down among the flowers
    Among the plants of – – – – – –
To Ltpn, God of Mercy.   (:45
Lo in my mouth is their number
    On my lips, their counting.
Her dowry
    And her trousseau
– – – – – to(ward) – – – – –
– – – – – to(ward) – – – – –
The fairest, the youngest of the Kosharot.   (:50

The *Epic of Kret* opens with the *Krt* text that tells how Kret's destined wife has been taken from him before she has given him an heir. Kret reaches El through incubation and implores the god to help him get the lady back so that he may have her, and through her, children to carry on his line. El tells Kret exactly what to do: what sacrifices to make, what

[53] The passive construction is clumsy here. The wording of this poem is so awkward that some scholars believe it was translated from a foreign language, perhaps Hurrian.

to prepare for the march to rescue his destined bride, what to do on reaching Udum, where the lady is being held by King Pbl, and so on. Kret follows El's orders but apparently later fails to fulfill a vow that he makes to Asherah in the course of his journey to Udum. By obeying El's instructions, Kret gets the lady, and their homecoming (text 128) is celebrated by a feast in Kret's palace, attended by the gods. El blesses the union by predicting that the lady (Ḥurrai) will bear Kret seven sons and an eighth child, a girl to be called Octavia. Among the sons will be Yaṣṣib, whom the goddesses will suckle to qualify him for kingship after Kret's reign. All the promised children are subsequently born, but Kret neglects to pay what he owes to Asherah. Text 128 closes with a description of Ḥurrai conducting a feast for Kret and his grandees. But text 125 continues the story, narrating how Kret falls ill (because he has failed to do what he vowed to Asherah) and faces death. The family is saddened and perplexed by the thought that Kret, who is believed to be El's son, could die. Kret tells a devoted son, Ilḥu by name, to stop grieving and instead summon Octavia to cure him. She apparently tries, but fails, to restore him to health. Kret's decrepitude has meanwhile brought dearth and famine to the land (text 126). Since human agency has not been able to heal Kret, the gods intercede. El asks for a divine volunteer, but finding none, himself undertakes to heal Kret by magic. Text 127 describes Kret's cure and return to his throne. At this juncture Yaṣṣib comes to Kret and tells him to get off the throne since he has been neglecting the duties of king during his long illness. Yaṣṣib claims the right to rule in his father's stead, then and there. For this presumption, Kret heaps a mighty malediction upon Yaṣṣib.

[Pertaining to K]ret.[54]   (Krt: 1
(*three lines broken*)
[   ] El [   ]   (:5
[   ] of the river, mothers
[   ] female shades.
Destroyed is the house of the [k]ing
Who had seven brothers
   Eight sons of one mother.
Kret, our scion, is improvished   (:10
   Kret, despoiled of a place.
His rightful wife he could not get

[54] This line labels the text, telling us that the ancients called it "Kret."

Nor his destined bride.
A woman did he bethroth
  But she departed.
Siblings germane were to be his: (:15
(But) a third die *at birth*
  A fourth, of disease
    A fifth Reshef gathers in
      A sixth are youths (victims) of the sea   (:20
        A seventh, lo they fall by the sword.
Kret sees his progeny
  He sees his progeny impoverished
    Greatly despoiled, his seat and house.
Lo a family is perished
  And in his castle (perished is) an heir.   (:25
He enters his chamber, he weeps
  While uttering words, shed tears
His tears are poured
  Like shekels earthward
    Like fifth-shekels on the bed.   (:30
As he weeps, he falls asleep
  As he sheds tears, slumber
    Yea sleep overcomes him
And he lies down in slumber
  And (then) is startled.   (:35
And in his dream El descends
  In his vision the Father of Man.[55]
And he draws near while asking Kret:
"Who is Kret that he should weep
  The Good One, Lad of El, that he should shed tears?   (:40
Does he wish the kingship of [Th]or, his Father?
  Or sovereignty, li[ke the Fa]ther of M[an]?
(*ten lines missing*)
A portion of her estate
  An eternal slave   (:55
A team of three horses
  A chariot from the yard of a handmaid's son.
[   ] I shall obtain
[   ] *exalt*, I'll increase

[55] Ugaritic calls man "Adam," exactly as in Hebrew.

[   ] Thor, his father, El
[   ] in weeping, Kret   (:60
   In shedding tears, the Good One, Lad of El:
Thou shalt wash
   And rouge thyself!
Wash thy hands to the elbow
   From thy fingers to the shoulder!
Enter [the shade of the tent]!   (:65
Take a lam[b in thy hands]
   A lamb of sa[crifice in] the right
     A kid in b[oth]
Loaves of [thy] b[read] of – – –
Take the entr[ails] of a bird of sacrifice   (:70
Po[ur] wine [from a c]up of silver
   Honey from a cup of [g]old
And rise to the top of the [to]wer
   Ride the shoulders of the wal[l]   (:75
Lift thy hands heavenward
   Sacrifice to Thor, thy Father, El
Bring Baal down with thy sacrifices
   Dagon's Son with thy victuals!
And let Kret go down from the roof.   (:80
Prepare food for the city
   Wheat for the House of Ḫbr [56]
Bake bread of the fifth
   Provisions of the sixth month.   (:85
The multitude is noble [57]
   And the army goes forth
     A noble army,
And there goes forth the multitude of *rank-and-file* [58]
   Thine army, a great host:
Three hundred myriads.
Troops without number   (:90
   Soldiers without reckoning.
Behold *ḫdd*-troops by the thousands

---

[56] Kret's city is not Ugarit, but Ḫbr, as we shall note again below.
[57] This translation of *ngb* (favored by T. Gaster and A. Goetze on account of Hittite evidence) is supported by Arabic *naǧib*, "noble."
[58] Conjectural translation, based on the assumption that this word contrasts with "noble," forming a pair of antonyms to express totality.

And *kmyr*-troops by the myriads.
Arrayed in twos
  Lo all of them arrayed in threes!   (:95
Let the solitary man close his house
  The widow indeed be hired
The invalid carry the bed [59]
  The one-eyed indeed – – – –   (:100
Let the newly wed groom come forth
  To drive his wife to another
    To a stranger his well-beloved [60]
Like locusts they shall occupy the field,

                                                                                            61

  Like grasshoppers the corners of the desert.   (:105
Go a day and a second
  A third, a fourth day
    A fifth, a sixth day
      Lo at sunrise on the seventh
Thou wilt reach Great Udum
  And Little Udum.[62]
And occupy the towns   (:110
  Invest the cities
Capture the man gathering wood in the fields
  The woman picking straw on the threshing floors
Capture the woman who draws at the well
  Who fills at the spring!
Then a day and a second
  A third day, a fourth day   (:115
    A fifth day, a sixth day
Do not send aloft thine arrows toward the city
  (Nor) the slingshot of thy hands
And behold at sunrise on the seventh
  King Pbl will not be sleeping   (:120

[59] In a national emergency, everyone must serve. While the invalid is not really well, he must at least try to act well and carry his bed.

[60] Even the newly wed groom must join the army. Accordingly, he disposes of his bride.

[61] This line is a scribal error because it comes between two parallel hemistichs. As the repetition of this section below will confirm, the line does not belong here.

[62] The "Little" city is the acropolis or fortified area containing the palace and temple. The "Great" city includes all the neighborhoods.

At the sound of the bellowing of his bull
At the voice of the braying of his ass
At the lowing of his plowing ox
The barking of his hunting dog
He will send messengers (saying):
'Go to Kret
Declare to him: (:125
"So says King Pbl:
'Take silver
Even gold
A share of her estate
And a permanent slave
A team of three horses
A chariot from the yard of a handmaid's son   (:130
Take, Kret, peace offerings in peace
And depart, King, from my house
Be distant, Kret, from my court!
Do not besiege Great Udum
And Little Udum   (:135
Udum is a gift of El
A present of the Father of Man.' " '
And send the messengers back to him (saying):
'What use have I for silver
Even of gold
A share of her estate
And a permanent slave   (:140
A team of three horses
A chariot from the yard of a handmaid's son?
But what is not in my house shalt thou give!
Give me Lady Ḥurrai
The fairest of thy firstborn's family [63]
Whose charm is like Anath's charm   (:145
Whose loveliness is like Astarte's loveliness,
Whose brows are lapis lazuli
Eyes, bowls of alabaster!
Let her gird me [   ]

[63] This interpretation would make Pbl's son the abductor of Ḥurrai. Another possible translation of the line is "The fair of family, thy firstborn," making Ḥurrai the noble firstborn of Pbl.

That I may repose in the view of the eyes of her
Whom El granted in my dream   (:150
   In my vision, the Father of Man,
That a scion be born unto Kret
   Yea a lad to the Servant of El.' "
Kret awakes, and 'twas a dream
   The Servant of El, and 'twas a theophany.   (:155
He washes
   Yea rouges himself
He washes his hands to the elbow
   From his fingers to the shoulder.
He enters into the shade of a tent
He takes a lamb of sacrifice in his hands   (:160
   A kid in both hands
Loaves of his bread of/which – – –
He takes the entrails of a bird of sacrifice
He pours wine from a cup of silver
   Honey from a cup of gold
And he goes up to the top of the tower   (:165
   He rides the shoulders of the wall
He lifts his hands unto heaven
He sacrifices to Thor, his father, El
   He brings Baal down with his sacrifices
      Dagon's Son with his victuals.   (:170
Kret goes down from the roof
He prepares food for the city
   Wheat for the House of Ḫbr
He bakes bread of the fifth
   Provisions of the sixth month.   (:175
The multitude is noble
   And [the army goes forth]
      A noble army,
[And there goes forth the multitude] of *rank-and-file*
   His army, a gr[eat host]:
Three hundred myriads.
Behold by thousands *ḫdd*-troops   (:180
   Yea, by the myriads, *kmyr*-troops
Arrayed in twos
   Lo all of them arrayed in threes.

The solitary man closes his house
   The widow indeed is hired   (:185
The invalid carries the bed
   The one-eyed indeed – – –
And the newly wed groom is brought forth
   To drive his wife to another   (:190
      Even to a stranger his well-beloved.
Like locusts they occupy the field
   Like grasshoppers the corners of the desert.
They go a day and a second   (:195
   After sunrise on the third
They r[each] Qdš [64]
   A [sherah] of the Tyrians
      The Goddess of the Sidonians
There Kret of Tha^c makes a vow: (:200
"As Asherah of the Tyrians lives
   Even the Goddess of the Sidonians!
If I may take Ḥurrai to my house
   Yea cause the girl to enter my court
I'll give twice her (price) in silver   (:205
   Even thrice her (price) in gold!"
They go a day and a second
   A third, a fourth day
      After sunrise on the fourth
They reach Great Udum   (:210
   And Little Udum.
He occupies the towns
   Invests the cities
Captures the man gathering wood in the field
   And the woman picking straw on the threshing floors.   (:215
Captures the woman who draws at the spring
   And her who fills at the well.
Then a day and a second
   A third, a fourth day
      A fifth, a sixth day   (:220
         Lo at the sunrise on the seventh
King Pbl could not sleep

[64] *Qdš*, "Holiness," can be one of the names of Asherah or, alternatively, a common noun meaning "shrine."

For the sound of the bellowing of his bull
  For the voice of the braying of his ass   (:225
    [For the lowing] of his plowing ox
      The barking of his hunting dog.
[Thereup]on [King] Pbl cries aloud to [his] wife:
"Hear, O [   ]!
  Wife [   ]:   (:230
The message [   ]
(*two lines broken*)
[   ] verily/not prepared
[   ] slingshot of his hands   (:235
[   ] shall I not send
[   ] aloud [to his lads] he cries:
[*hit*]*ch an ass*
(*three lines broken*)   (:240
[   ] sacrifice
(*three lines broken*)   (:245
"[Go] to [Kret of Tha]ᶜ!
And s[ay to Kret of Thaᶜ]:
'The message [of King Pbl]:
"Take [silver]   (:250
  [Even go]ld
A [share] of her [estate]
  An [eternal] slave
[A team of three] hor[ses]
  [A chariot] from [the yard of a handmaid's son]!
[Take, Kret, peace offerings in peace!   (:255
Do not besiege Great Udum
  And Little Udum
Udum is the gift of El
  Yea a present of the Father of Man.
So depart, O King, from my] house
  [Be distant, Kre]t, from my c[ou]rt!" ' "   (:260
(*five lines missing*)
They l[ift their voices
  And shout]:
"The messa[ge of King Pbl]:
'Take si[lver
  Even go]ld   (:270

[A share of her estate]
 And an [eternal] slave
[A team of three] horses
 [A chariot] from the yard [of a handmaid's son]!
Ta[ke], Kret, [peace offerings in] pea[ce]!   (:275
Do not [besiege] Great Udum
 And [Lit]tle U[dum]!
Udum is a gift of El
 A present of the Father of [Ma]n.
Be distant, King, from my house
 Depart, Kret, from [my] cour[t]!' "   (:280
And [K]ret of [Tha]ᶜ answered:
"What use have I for silver
 Even go[ld]
A share of her estate
 An eternal slave   (:285
A team of three horses
 A chariot from the yard of a handmaid's son?
But what is not in my house shalt thou give!
Give me Lady Ḥurrai
 The fairest of thy firstborn's family   (:290
Whose charm is like Anath's charm
 Whose loveliness is like Astarte's loveliness
Whose brows are lapis lazuli
 Eyes, bowls of alabaster.   (:295
Whom El has given in my dream
 In my vision the Father of Man:
So that a scion may be born unto Kret
 Yea a lad, to the servant of El!"
The messengers depart
 They do not sit
Then they set face toward King Pbl.
They lift their voices
 And shout:
"The message of Kret of Thaᶜ
 The word of the [G]ood One, [Lad of El]:"
(*rest missing*)
[   ] hand [   ]   (128:I:1
 The thirsty by the hand she took

She caused him to – – – [   ] *in judgment*
To Kret *say as follows:*
"As the cow moos to her calf   (:5
  So do the sons of soldiery (cry) to their mothers
    As the Udumites groan."
And Kret of Tha^c replies:

[   ]   (128:II:1
[   ] Thor
[Ali]yan Baal
[   ] Moon, the Prince
[   ] Kothar-and-Ḥasis   (:5
[   ] Raḥmay, Reshef the prince
The [asse]mbly of the gods threefold.
There[upon] Kret of Tha^c
Puts – – – – in his house
He enters his [   ]
He gives and [   ] gives [   ]   (:10
There arrives the assembly of the gods
[And] Ali[yan] Baal declares:
"[   ] depart, O Lṭpn, [God] of Mercy,
Wilt thou not bless [Kret] of Tha^c   (:15
  Nor protect the Good One, [Lad] of El?"
A cup he takes [in] (his) hand [65]
  A goblet in [the right]
El indeed blesses Kret [of Tha^c]
  [Protects] the Good One, Lad of El: (:20
"The wi[fe thou take]st, O Kret,
  The wife thou takest to thy house
    The girl thou causest to enter thy court
Will bear thee seven sons
And an eighth (daughter): Octavia.
To thee she will bear the lad Yaṣṣib   (:25
  One who sucks the milk of Asherah

---

[65] Benediction with a cup of wine is very ancient and widespread. It is commonly depicted on Mesopotamian seal cylinders of the Ur III dynasty (*ca.* 2000 B.C.).

Who suckles the breasts of the Virgin [Anath]
The wetnurs[es of the Good and Fair Gods].

[   ]   (128:III:1
  [Be most exalted], O Kret!
[In the midst of the deities] of the earth
  [In the gathering] of the assembly of Dtn.
[And she] will come to term to bear   (:5
[   ] she will go
She will bear the Girl
  She will bear the Gir[l   ]
    She will bear the Gir[l   ]
She will bear the Gi[rl   ]   (:10
  She will bear the Gi[rl   ]
    She will bear the Gi[rl   ]
Be most exalted, [O Kret]!
In the midst of the deities of the ear[th]
  In the gathering of the assembly of Dtn.   (:15
I shall make the youngest of them the firstborn." [66]
The gods bless, they go
  The gods go to their tents
    The assembly of El to their tabernacles.
And she comes to term to bear him a son   (:20
  And she comes to term to bear him two sons.
Lo! in seven years
The sons of Kret were as she had promised
  Also the daughters of Ḥurrai were so.
And Asherah is mindful of her vows   (:25
  Yea the Goddess [of her promises]
And she lifts her voice
  And [shouts]:
"Look! Will Kret even [break his word]
  Or [   ] change [his] vows?
I shall break [then my agreement]."   (:30

---

[66] A younger child could be made "fratriarch," or chief, over his older siblings
(I Chronicles 26:10). In our Ugaritic text, the "youngest" is feminine; thus
Octavia is to be "sororarch"; see I Chronicles 7:18 in the original Hebrew
for "sororarch" (literally, "ruling sister").

[   ]
[He sets his] fe[et on the footstool]   (128:IV:1
Aloud [he shouts] to [his wife]:
"Hear, [O Lady Ḥurrai]!
Slaught[er] the sleeke[st] of thy fatlings!   (:5
   Open a fl[a]gon of wine!
Invite my seventy bulls
   My eighty gazelles
The bulls of [Gre]at Ḫbr
   Of L[it]tle Ḫbr
(*four lines broken*)   (:10
Lady Ḥurrai hearkens.
She slaughters the sleekest of her [fat]lings   (:15
She opens a flagon of wine
Into his presence she ushers his bulls
   Into his presence she ushers his gazelles [67]
The bulls of Great Ḫbr
   Of Little Ḫbr.   (:20
They enter the house of Kret
   To [his] dwelling [they come]
   They proceed to the – – – – – – .
She stretches a hand into the bowl
   A knife she puts into the meat.   (:25
[And] Lady Ḥurrai announces:
"I have invited you [to ea]t, to drink
   Kret, your lord, [has a feast]."
(*five lines broken*)   (128:V:1
[   ] dwelling [   ]   (:6
[She stret]ches a hand into the bowl
   She puts [a knife] into the meat
[And] Lady Ḥurrai [announces]:
"I have invited you [to ea]t, to drink   (:10
[   ] bless [   ]
Ye shall weep [over] Kret.
[Even as] the bulls had said
[   ] the dead, ye shall weep
[   ] and in the heart ye shall *bu[ry*   ]   (:15
[   ] dead, finger[s   ]."

    [67] "Bulls" and "gazelles" may be conventional terms for Kret's barons.

[   ] – – – – – El, sunset
   Verily Kret reaches the setting sun
Our lord, and he rules
[   ] our lord and he [   ]   (:20
[Kre]t of Thaᶜ upon us in Ḫr
[   ] thy wife on
[   ] he causes to go out
[   ] Great Ḫbr   (:25
[Littl]e [Ḫbr].
[   ]
[   ] full
[   ] complete
Hear [   ] – – – – – [   ] – – –   (128:VI:1
They are still e[atin]g (and) drinking
And Lady Ḫurrai announces:
"I have invited you to e[a]t (and) to dr[ink]
   [Kret], your lord, [has] a fea[st]."   (:5
Into the presence of Kret they come
As the bulls had said
   Their word in the vision [   ] Kret
[   ]
   Kret [   ]   (125:1
"Like a [d]og in thy house do we slink
   Like a cur, (in) thy bower.
Father, wilt even thou die like mortals [68]
   Nor we be allowed to pass through thy bower   (:5
     By the women, O Father, in the heights
        (Who) mourn thee, Father, in the mountain of Baal Saphon?
The holy dirge is loud
   A mighty dirge
     A dirge, wide of wing.
Also, is [K]ret a son of El   (:10
The scion of Lṭpn-and-Qdš?" [69]
Into the presence of his father he enters
He weeps and gnashes teeth for him
   He gives forth his voice, in weeping:

---

[68] *Cf.* Psalm 82:7: "Will ye die like a man, and fall like one of the princes?"
[69] Lṭpn is El, Qdš ("Holiness") apparently refers to Asherah. Kret was accordingly accepted as the son of the chief god and goddess.

"In thy life, O our father, would we rejoice
   Thine immortality, we would be glad therein!   (:15
Like a dog in thy house do we slink
   Like a cur, (in) thy bower.
O Father, wilt thou also die like mortals?
   Nor we be allowed to pass through thy bower
      By the women, O Father, in the heights?
How can it be said   (:20
Kret is El's son
   The scion of Lṭpn-and-Qdš?
Or do gods die
   Nor Lṭpn's scion live?"
And Kret of Thaᶜ replies:
"My son, do not weep for me   (:25
   Do not grieve for me!
Do not exhaust, O my son, the well of thine eyes
   Nor the water [70] of thy head with tears!
Summon thy sister Octavia
      From the house of her *guardian*, Danan,   (:30
         So that she may weep and mourn for me.
My lad, do not tell thy sister
[   ] thy sister.
I know that she is kind
Let her not put her waters in the field
   Nor the outpouring of her soul in the meadow.   (:35
[When] Lady Sun will be setting
   Yea the Lady gleaming with glow
Then say to thy sister Octavia:
'Kretan [71] is making a feast   (:40
   The king is giving a party
Take thy – – – in the hand
   Thy – – – in the right.
Go, abide on the heights of thy sire
Cause [   ] to draw near with thy gifts   (:45
   And he will agree to everything.' "
Thereupon the hero Ilḫu

---

[70] Reading *my* (for *mḫ*), as proposed by S. Gevirtz. In Ugaritic cuneiform, *y* and *ḫ* are sometimes confused.

[71] This is the longer form of "Kret" (i.e., with the suffix *-an*).

Takes his [l]ance in the hand
   His [sp]ear in the right
[   ] he draws near running to her
   [   ] he reaches her.   (:50
And the lad *attracts the attention of* his sister
   And she goes out and [espies] his lance
He sets his face
   Goes out of the door.
As soon as she sees her brother
She breaks her [back] on the earth
[   ] her brother, she weeps   (:55
[   ] "Is the king [s]ick
   [   ] is Kret, thy sire, [ill]?"
And the hero Ilḥu [replies]:
"The king is [not] sick
   [Nor ill is K]ret, thy sire.   (:60
[Kretan is m]aking a feast
   [The king is g]iving a party."
(*twelve lines broken*)
and she shouts [   ]   (:75
she gives drink [   ]
– – – – [   ]
and a mixture – – [   ]
she nears [her] brother [and asks]:
"Why dost thou beguile me?   (:80
How many months is it that Kret is si[ck]
   How many that Kret is ill?"
And the hero [Ilḥu] replies:
"Three months that he is sick
   Four that K[ret] is ill."   (:85
Whether Kret has arri[ved   ]
And the grave, will besiege [   ]
It will besiege, be high, *slumber* [   ]
Like the – – – – – of the gate [   ]
   Like the completion [   ]   (:90
– – – – not to [   ]
[   ] reply [   ]
not to – – – and [   ]
her brother-in-law, seven [   ]

the hero Ilḥu [   ]   (:95
will be high, will besiege, will be high [   ]
She weeps and she g[nashes teeth   ]
   [She gives forth] her voice in weeping:
"In thy life, O our [fa]ther, would we rejoice
   Thine immortality, we would be glad therein.
Like a dog in thy house do we slink   (:100
   Like a cur in thy bower
Wilt also thou, O Father, die like mortals
   Or thy bower pass to weeping
      By the women, O Father, in the heights?   (:105
Or do gods die?
   Nor Ltpn's scion live?
The mountains of Baal Saphon will weep for thee, O Father
The holy dirge is loud
   The mighty [dir]ge
      The dirge wide of w[ing].
Is Kret then a son [of El]   (:110
   The scion of Ltpn-[and-Qdš]?"
Weeping she enters [   ]
   She enters [his] cha[mber   ]
In two [   ]
She abides [   ]   (:115
weepers [   ]
mountain [   ]
(*rest broken*)
He pours oil [   ]   (126:III:1
a well [   ] earth and heavens
The way(s) of the trees of the earth
for *spelt* – – – of the well
For the earth, the r[ai]n of Baal   (:5
   Yea for the field, the rain of the Good Exalted One.
For the earth, the rain of Baa[l]
   Yea for the field the rain of the Good Exalted One.
For the wheat, in the well, in the tillage   (:10
   Spelt on [   ] *perfumes*.
The plowmen lifted the head
   On top of the [   ] Dagon.
Spent is the bread [from] their jars

Spent is the wine from their bottles (:15
   Sp[e]nt is the oil from [their] c[ruses].
They [enter] the house of Kret.
(*about three lines missing*)
[   ] El: (126:IV:1
"Listen, I shall protect thee
Look [   ] like El
   Thou art wise like Thor-Ltpn,
Call the carpenter god Ilš
   Ilš and his wives the carpenter goddesses. (:5
   Like – – – – – – [   ]."
He calls the carpenter god, Ilš
   Ilš the carpenter of the house of Baal
      And his wives the carpenter goddesses.
And Ltpn, God of Mercy, declares: (:10
"Hear, O Carpenter God, Ilš
   Ilš the carpenter of the house of Baal
      And thy wives, the carpenter goddesses!
Go up to the shoulders of the buildings
– – – – – – – – – – (:15
The three of you, my *little ones*
[   ] to the mountain – – – – – [   ]
(*about thirty-seven lines broken*)
In thy hands [   ] (126:V:7
A second time [   ]
   A third time [   ]
Ltpn, [God of Mercy, declares]: (:10
"[Who] among the gods [will drive out the disease]
   Exorcizing the i[llness]?"
[None among the gods] answers him.
A [fourth time] he says:
"Who among [the gods will drive out] the disease (:15
   Exorciz[ing the illness]?"
None among the gods an[swers him].
A fifth time he says:
"[Who among the gods] will drive out the disease
   Ex[orcizing the illness]?"
None among the gods answer[s him].
A sixth, a seventh time he says: (:20

"[Who] among the gods will drive out the disease
   Exorcizing the illness?"
None among the gods answers him,
And Ltpn, God of Mercy, declares:
"Return, my sons, to your seat[s]
   Yea to the thrones of yo[ur] excellencies!   (:25
I will perform magic
   Verily to stay the hand of the disease
      Exorcizing the illness."
[   ] fills
The Good One shapes [   ] clay
– – – – – [   ] – – –   (:30
[   ] Tannin
   [   ] Tannin
(*rest broken*)
"[De]ath, then, be stilled!   (127:1
   Š^etqt [72] then, prevail!"
And Š^etqt departed.
She verily enters the house of Kret
   Weeping she goes in and enters
      Sobbing she comes inside.   (:5
The towns she enters – –
   The cities she enters – – –
With a wand *she strikes* the malady
   The illness on its head.
And she returns to wash him of sweat.   (:10
His appetite she opens to eat
   His desire to dine.
Death, then, is stilled.
   Š^etqt, then, prevails over him.
And Kret of Tha^c gives orders   (:15
   He lifts his voice
      And shouts:
"Hear, O Lady Ḫurrai!
Slaughter a lamb that I may eat
   A lambkin that I may dine!"
Lady Ḫurrai hearkens
She slaughters a lamb that he may eat   (:20

_____
[72] This name means "she who causes (illness) to pass."

A lambkin that he may dine.
Lo a day and a second
Kret returns to his audience hall
   He sits on the throne of his kingship
      On the dais, on the chair of sovereignty.
Also Yaṣṣib returns to the palace   (:25
   And his inwards instruct him:
"Go to thy father, Yaṣṣib,
   Go [to] thy [fa]ther and speak!
      Repeat to K[ret of Thaᶜ]:
'Liste[n]
   And be alert [of ear]!   (:30
For dost thou administer like the *strongest* of the *strong*
   And govern (like) the [moun]tains?
Thou hast let thy hands fall into negligence
Thou dost not judge the case of the widow
   Nor adjudicate the cause of the broken in spirit.[73]
Because thou art a brother of the bed of sickness   (:35
   Yea a companion of the bed of disease.
Descend from the kingship that I may rule
   From thy sovereignty, that I may be enthroned thereon!' "
The lad Yaṣṣib departs
   Into his father's presence he enters.   (:40
He lifts his voice
   And shouts:
"Hear, O Kret of Thaᶜ!
   Listen
      And be alert of ear!
Dost thou administer like the *strongest* of the *strong*
   And govern (like) the mountains?
Thou hast let thy hands fall into negligence   (:45
Thou dost not judge the case of the widow
   Nor adjudicate the cause of the broken in spirit
      Nor drive away those who *prey* upon the poor!
Before thee thou dost not feed the fatherless
   Nor behind thy back the widow.[74]   (:50

[73] The traditional duty of the kings was to rescue the helpless and weak.
[74] This is a twofold "inclusive expression." "Before" and "behind" in combination mean "on all sides"; "fatherless" and "widow" in combination denote all kinds of unfortunate people in need of the king's protection.

For thou art a brother of the bed of sickness
  Yea a companion of the bed of disease.
Descend from the kingship that I may rule
  From thy sovereignty that I may be enthroned thereon!"
And Kret of Tha^c replies:
"May Ḫoron break, O my son,   (:55
  May Ḫoron break thy head
    Astarte-Name-of-Baal, thy pate!
May there fall in Byblos
  Thy years in thy − − −
And mayest thou see [   ]."
The scribe is Elimelech, the Tha^cite.[75]   (:left edge

The *Epic of Aqhat* opens with the righteous King Danel offering
sacrifices and libations to the gods for six days so that he may be blessed
with a model son. Then he engages in incubation, so that Baal appears
to him on the seventh day. King Danel makes his request and on receiving divine blessing, goes to his wife and impregnates her. In due time
the model son is born, and the Kosharot are invited to Danel's palace,
where they are wined and dined for a week. One day while Danel is
judging the cause of the widow and the orphan, Kothar-and-Ḫasis brings
a wondrous bow for Aqhat, the son. Danel's wife, Danatay, serves a feast
to Kothar-and-Ḫasis before he returns to his tents. Aqhat becomes such a
famous hunter with his divinely fashioned bow that Anath, the huntress,
covets it. She offers him wealth for the bow, but he refuses it. She then
offers him immortality for it, and again he refuses, adding that he does
not trust her, and that anyway as a female she should leave bowmanship
to men. For the affront, Anath extorts permission from El to bring violence
to Aqhat. She then secures the services of Yaṭpan to smite Aqhat while
the latter is lunching in the open during a hunt. A flock of eagles are on
the scene, and one of them devours the slain Aqhat. The death of such
a hero brings drought and famine on the land. The parched crops tell
the story. Then Aqhat's sister Pughat sights the eagles and divines the
tragedy. Danel and Pughat go into mourning. Danel curses the land with
a cycle of drought. Pughat then mounts her father on a donkey, and he

[75] Here Elimelech is called a member of the Tha^c tribe; above, a scribe of
the same name was called a member of the Šbn tribe.

rides off to curse the spot where the crime was perpetrated. Knowing
more or less what has happened, Danel invokes Baal to bring down the
eagle who has swallowed Aqhat's remains.[76] Danel retrieves the remains
for burial. Seven years of mourning, with the help of wailing women, are
observed in Danel's palace. Then Pughat, dressed as a man, with a weapon
concealed under her clothing, gains access to Yaṭpan, whom she apparently kills. The sequel (including the revival of Aqhat) is not pre-
served on the tablets found thus far.

(several lines missing)

The gods will eat the offerings   (2 Aqhat:I:1 [77]
   The deities [will drink the offerings].

He proceeds, [ascends to his *loft*]   (:5
   And he lies down

He proceeds [   ] spends the night.

Lo a day [and a second]
   [The offerings], the gods, Danel!
     [The gods] eat the [offerings]
       The deities [drink] the offerings.

A third, a fourth day
   [The offerings, the g]ods, Danel!   (:10
     [The gods] eat the offerings
       The de[ities] drink the offerings.

A [f]ifth, a sixth day
   The offerings, [the gods], Danel!
     The gods eat the offerings
       The deities drink the [offerings].

[Dan]el proceeds to his *loft*   (:15
   He proceeds to his *loft* (and) ascends
     And he lies down [clad in] a garb
       And spends the night.

Baal drew near while he supplicated (and Baal said):

---

[76] The text achieves an atmosphere of suspense by telling how Danel first
brings down the flock of eagles without retrieving Aqhat's remains; then he
brings down the father of the eagles, but again in vain. Only on the third try,
when he brings down the mother of the eagles, does he find Aqhat's remains
for burial.

[77] We follow the number of Virolleaud's original edition in order to facilitate
checking against the cuneiform. The plot requires that "1 Aqhat" follow "2 and
3 Aqhat."

"The wretchedness of [Da]nel, Man of Rp²,[78]
  The sigh of the Hero, [Man] of Hrnmy,
Who has no son like his brothers   (:20
  Nor a root like his kinsmen!
Indeed he possesses no son like his brothers
  Nor a root like his kinsmen!
The gods eat the offerings
  The deities drink the offerings.
Will they not bless him to Thor-El, my father,
  Nor defend him to the Creator of Creatures   (:25
So that a son of his may be in the house
  A root in the midst of his palace?
One who sets up the stela of his ancestral gods in the shrine
  Who *lays* his people *to rest* on the earth
    Sends out his incense from the dust
The soldier of his post
  Who heaps the tablets of his *office*   (:30
    Expels him who *eats the supper of his spending the night*
Who takes his hand in drunkenness
  Who carries him [when] sated with wine
Who eats his meal in the house of Baal
  His [por]tion in the house of El
Who plasters his roof on the day of [mu]d [79]
  Who washes his clothes on the day of slime."
[   ] El takes his servant.   (:35
He blesses [Dane]l, Man of Rp²,
  Protects the Hero, [Man of H]rnmy:
"By my soul, may Danel, [Man of Rp]², live
  By my spirit, the Hero, Man of Hrnmy!
[   ] may he prosper!"
On his couch he ascends
[   ] in kissing his wife   (:40
[   ] in embracing her, childbirth
[   ] bearing, childbirth [   ]
So that his son will be [in the house
  A root] in the midst of his palace

  [78] The root *rp²* can refer to the shades of the dead or to healing. It is possible that Danel was credited with curative powers and was therefore called "the man of healing."
  [79] The good son would plaster his father's roof with the mud that was available after a rain.

[One who sets up the stela of his an]cestral gods in the shrine (:45
  [Who *lays* his people *to rest* on the e]arth
    Sends out [his incense from the dust]
[The so]ldier of his p[o]st
  Who heaps the tablets of his *office*
    [Expels] him who *eats the supper of his spending the night*
(*several lines missing*)
Who la[*ys to rest* thy people on earth] (2 Aqhat: II:1
  [Sends out thine incense] from the dust
The soldi[er of thy post
  Who heaps] the tablets of thine *office*
    Expe[ls him who *eats the supper of thy spending the night*]
Who eats thy meal in the house [of Baal]
  [Thy portion] in the house of El. (:5
Who takes thy hand in [drunkenness]
  Who carries thee when thou art sated with wine
Plas[ters] thy roof on the day of mud
  Washes thy clothes on the day of slime."
On Dane[l], the face rejoices
  Yea above, the temp[le] gleams.
He cracks a smile (:10
  And laughs.
Feet on the footstool he sets.
He lifts his voice
  And shouts:
"I shall [s]it and rest
  And my soul shall repose in my breast
For a son is born unto me like my brothers (:15
  Even a root like my kin:
One who sets up the stela of my ancestral gods in the shrine
  Lays to rest my people on the dust
The soldier of [my] post
  Who heaps the tablets of mine *office*
    Expels him who *eats the supper of my spending the night*
Who takes my hand in drunkenness (:20
  Who carries me when I'm sated with wine
Who eats my meal in Baal's house
  My [portion] in the house of El
Plasters my roof on the day of mud
  Washes my clothes on the day of slime."

Danel goes to his house
> Danel reaches his palace.   (:25
There enter his house the Kosharot
> The daughters of shouting, the swallows.
Thereupon Danel, Man of Rp',
> Straightway the hero, Man of Hrnmy,
Slaughters an ox for the Kosharot   (:30
He feeds the Kosharot
> He gives the daughters of sho[ut]ing, the swallows, to drink.
Lo a day and a second
> He feeds the Kosharot
>> And gives the daughters of shouting, the swallows, to dr[in]k.
A third, a fourth day
> He feeds the Kosharot   (:35
>> And gives the daughters of shouting, the swallows, to drink.
A fifth, a sixth day
> He feeds the Kosharot
>> And gives the daughters of shouting, the swallows, to [drink].
Lo on the seventh day
> There depart from his house the Kosharot   (:40
>> The daughters of shouting, the swallows.
> [   ] the beauty of the couch [   ]
>> [   ] the loveliness of the couch [   ]
Danel returns [   ]
> [   ]
A third, a fourth [   ]   (:45
month, he reaches [   ]
(two lines broken)
"I bring a bow   (2 Aqhat:V:2
> I fetch an arc."
And behold on the seve[nth] day
Thereupon Danel, Man of Rp',   (:5
> Straightway the Hero, Man of Hrnmy,
Picks himself up
> Yea he sits
In the enclosure of the gate [80]

---

[80] Ancient city gates often had an enclosure for official proceedings. "Threshing floor," in the next line, designates the place where court was held, as in other ancient Near East texts (C. H. Gordon, *Ugaritic Literature*, p. 84, n. 2).

Under the dignitaries which is in the threshing floor.
He judges the case of the widow
    Adjudicates the cause of the fatherless.
On lifting his eyes
    He perceives
By the thousand acres   (:10
    Myriad hectares
He spies the going of Kothar
    He spies the course of Ḥasis.[81]
Lo he brings a bow
    Behold he fetches an arc.
Thereupon Danel, Man of Rpʾ,
    Straightway the Hero, Man of Hrnmy,   (:15
Shouts aloud to his wife:
"Hear, Lady Danatay!
Prepare a lamb from the flock
For the soul of Kothar and Ḥasis
    For the appetite of the Skilled of Handicraft!
Feed, give drink to, the gods [82]   (:20
    Serve and honor them
      Lords of Ḥkpt
        Gods of all of it!" [83]
Lady Danatay hearkens
She prepares a lamb from the flock
For the soul of Kothar and Ḥasis
    The appetite of the Skilled of Handicraft.   (:25
After Kothar and Ḥasis come,
In the hands of Danel they set the bow
    On his knees they place the arc.

[81] My student Miss Alexandra Lambropoulou makes the acute observation that Minoan architecture fits this passage, which calls for the king to sit at a lower level than the nobles but to be able to see the approaching god. By the main entrance at both Knossos and Phaistos is an open court with tiered rows of seats for the nobles. The king, seated in front of them, would be at a lower level than the nobles, and facing the edge of the unwalled city with an excellent view for seeing the god approaching, even at a low flying altitude.

[82] Here Kothar and Ḥasis are treated as two gods, grammatically dual.

[83] "All" of a land is an idiom (found in the Northwest Semitic dialects, including Aramaic) designating all the provinces or divisions of a country. Here both parts of Ḥkpt are intended, i.e., Upper and Lower Egypt. Another possible translation is "Lords of all glorious Ḥkpt" with the word "god(s)" implying glory or splendor (*UT* §13:22, pp. 113–114).

Thereupon Lady Danatay
Feeds, gives drink to, the gods
   She serves and honors them   (:30
      Lords of Ḥkpt
         Gods of all of it.
Kothar departs to his tents
   The Skilled departs to his tabernacles.
Thereupon Danel, Man of Rpʾ,
   Straightway the Hero, Man of Hrnmy,   (:35
The bow he [   ]
[   ] upon Aqhat [   ]
"*Bag* thy quarry, O my son [   ]
   Bag thy quarry, lo [for]
Quarry, into his palace [   ]"
(*three lines broken*)   (2 Aqhat:VI:1
[With a] kee[n k]nife
   [A slice of fatling]
[They drink] wine [from a goblet]   (:5
   From a cup of gol[d, the blood of vines].
[   ] goblet on [   ] a day
And there goes up must
[   ] wine of *supper* from Ḥbš
[   ] – – – she answers – – – – [   ]
On lifting her eyes   (:10
   She sees
[   ] her back [   ]
[   ] – – – – – the deeps, lightning
[   ] the bow is set between [ ]
[   ] like a serpent he hisses
[   ] on the earth, garment – – – –   (:15
[She lifts her voice]
   And shouts:
"Hear, [O Aqhat the Hero!]
[Re]quest silver and I'll give thee
   [Gold, and I'll en]dow thee!
But give [me thy] bow
   Let the Progenitress of Heroes [ta]ke thine [a]rc!"
And Aqhat the Hero replies: (:20
"The mightiest sinews of Lebanon

The mightiest tendons from buffaloes
   The mightiest horns from wild goats
      The – – – – from the tendons of a bull
        The mightiest *stems* of reeds:
Give (such) to Kothar and Ḫasis
So that he may fashion a bow for her
   An arc for the Progenitress of Heroes."   (:25
And the Virgin Anath replies:
"Request life, O Aqhat the Hero!
   Request life and I'll give thee!
      Immortality and I'll endow thee!
I shall cause thee to count years with Baal
   With the son of El shalt thou count months
Like Baal as he lives!"   (:30
He pours out drinks, alive
   He pours out and gives her to drink.
The Good One chants
   Yea sings about her.
[And she] declares:
"I would even immortalize Aqha[t the Her]o!"
But Aqhat the Hero replies:
"Do not beguile me, O Virgin!
   For to a hero thy lies are loathsome!   (:35
As for man, what does he get as his destiny?
   What does man get as his fate?
Lime is poured [on] the head
   Plaster on top of my pate.[84]
[And] I'll die the death of everyone
   Yea I shall surely die!
[Also anoth]er thing I shall tell:
The bow [is a weapon of h]eroes   (:40
   Could a female really hunt [therewith]?"
Anath laughs [alo]ud
But in heart – – – [   ]:
"[Recon]sider, O Hero Aqhat,
   Reconsider for my sake and thine!

[84] As I have learned from Margaret Lee, this refers to the ancient funeral custom of plastering the pate of the deceased. Plastered skulls have been found at Jericho.

[Other]wise shall I not meet thee on the path of sin
   [Nor] fell thee on the path of pride
      Under [my feet], O Good One, strongest of men?"   (:45
[She jumps with the feet]
   And leaves earth.
Then [she sets fac]e toward El
At the sources of the Two Rivers
   [In the midst of the streams] of the Two Deeps.
She enters the abode of El
   [Comes into the do]micile of the king, Father of Šnm.
[At the feet of El she] bows and falls   (:50
   Prostrates [herself and honors him].
She slanders Aqhat the Hero
   [Maligns the child of Dan]el, Man of Rp'.
And [the Virgin Anath] declares
   [She lifts] her [voice]
      And shouts:
"The word [   ] Aqhat [   ]."
(*rest broken*)
And [the Virgin Anath] answers: (3 Aqhat:"rev.":6 [85]
"[   ] O gods [   ]
[   ] do not rej[oice   ]
[do not] be glad [   ]
[in] the greatness of [my] len[gth   ]   (:10
I shall make [thy gray hair] flow [with blood
   The gray of] thy [beard] with gore.
And [then] will Aqhat save thee
   Or will [Danel's] son rescue thee
      From the hand of the Virgin [Anath]?"
And Ltpn, God of Me[rcy], replies: (:15
"I know thee, my daughter, that thou art impetuous
   And there is n[o forbearance] among goddesses.
So depart, my daughter – – –
   Evil is [thy] heart [   ]
The joy that there is in thy liver
   Thou shalt put in [the midst] of thy breast.
Let thy heels surely thresh."

   [85] As labeled in the *editio princeps*, but actually this is the obverse and we accordingly place it before the other side.

The [Vir]gin Anath [laughs]   (:20
Then she sets [face toward] Aqhat the Hero
By the thousand acr[es]
    [Myriad] hectares.
And the Virgin [Anath] laughs
    [She lifts] her voice
        And shouts:
"Hear, [O Aqhat the Her]o!
Thou art my brother
    And I [am thy sister]!
[   ] thy seven relatives [   ]   (:25
[   ] my father
I have proceeded [   ] the king
    Thou shalt go on the hunt [   ]
[   ] man – – – – [   ]
    I shall teach thee [   ]
The City of Mourners, A[bilûma],[86]   (:30
    [The City of Prince M]oon.
For great [   ]
[   ] city [   ]
(*rest broken*)
[   ] he breaks [   ]   (3 Aqhat:"obv.":2 [87]
[   ] – – – – – [   ]
[The Virgi]n Anath to all [   ]
    The Virgin Anath [goes] to Yaṭpan, Soldier of the L[ady]   (:5
[She lifts her voice]
    And shouts:
"Let Yaṭp(an) return [   ]
The City of Mourners, Abilûma,
    [The City of Prince Moon].
How will he not renew the moon
[   ] with its right horn?   (:10
Savagely [thou shalt strike] his head."
And Yaṭpan, [Soldier of the Lady], replies:
"Hear, O Virgin Anath!
Wilt thou on [account of his bow]
    Smite him (for) his arc

[86] *Abilûma* means "mourners."
[87] Actually the reverse, as noted above.

(But) himself wilt thou not [let live]?
The Good One, the Hero, has set food
   And [poured] *oil* in the *area*   (:15
So that we shall – – – [   ]"
And the Virgin Anath declares:
"Reconsider, Yaṭpan, yea [reconsider, for my sake and] thine!
I shall make thee like an eagle with [my] shea[th]
   Like a bird with my scabbard.
Aqhat, [as he will sit down] to eat
   Yea the son of Danel to dine
[Over him] eagles will soar   (:20
   There will hover [a flight of b]irds
Among the eagles I shall be flying
   [Ove]r Aqhat I shall poise thee.
Strike him twice on the head
   Thrice over the ear!
Spill, like a slayer, blood
   Like a slaughterer, on his knees.
Let his soul go out like the wind   (:25
   Like a gust, his spirit
      Like smoke out of his nose!
But his *lad(s)* shall I not keep alive?"
She takes Yaṭpan, Soldier of the Lady,
   She makes him like an eagle with her sheath
      Like a bird with her scabbard.
As Aqhat sits down to ea[t]
   The son of Danel to dine   (:30
Over him eagle[s] soar
   There hovers a flight of bird[s.
Among] the eagles soars Anath
   Over [Aqhat] she poises him
He strikes him twice [on the head]
   Thrice over the ear.
He sp[ills like] a slayer his blood   (:35
   Like a slaughter[er on his knees].
[His] soul goes out like wind
   [Like a gust], his spirit
      Like smoke, [out of his nose].
Anath, as her soldier strikes Aqhat

[The Progenitress of Heroes] weeps [saying]:
"[Aqhat] I shall repair (:40
Yea for [the bow was he smitten]
   [Only indeed for] the arc
But thou shalt surely l[ive   ]"
And perished, flying [   ]
(*rest broken*)

Pertaining to Aqhat.[88] (1 Aqhat:1
[   ] to the midst [   ] waters
She falls [   ] heart
She br[ea]ks the bow [   ]
   He breaks eight [   ] (:5
The Virgin Anath returns/brea[ks   ]
[Li]fts mounds – – – [   ] her hands
Like the so[ng] of the harp of his fingers
   Like the whiteness of the stones of his mouth
She takes his teeth and the food in – – –
She whitens herself [89] like the heart of the gods (:10
And two – – – – – – – – – – – –
Aqhat, he answers/sees – – – – – –
for I appear, El, in the fences – – – for his staff
I smote him – – – on account of his bow
   I smote him on account of his arc (:15
      But him would I not keep alive?
Also his bow was not given to me
and – – – [   ] – – – – –
[   ] summer fruit – – – ear [in] its husk.
Thereupon Danel, [Ma]n of Rp', (:20
   Straig[ht]way the H[er]o, [Man of Hrn]my
Picks himself up
   [Sits in the enclosure of the g]ate
      [U]nder [the dignitaries who are on the threshing floor.]
[He] judges [the case of the widow]
Adjudicates [the cause of the fatherless] (:25
(*two and a half lines broken*)

[88] This title shows that the ancients named the story after Aqhat rather than Danel.

[89] Women painted themselves pale yellow or white, while men reddened their bodies. This is apparent from the art as well as the texts of the region, including Egypt and the Aegean.

[On lif]ting her eyes
  She sees [   ]
[   ] in the threshing floor it dries   (:30
He lowers, he – – – [   ]
Eagles fly over the house of her father
  There hovers a flight of birds.
Pughat weeps in her heart
  She sheds tears in the liver   (:35
She tears the garment of Danel, Man of Rp',
  The garb of the Hero, Man of Hrnmy.
Thereupon Danel, Man of Rp', prays:
"Clouds in the heat of the evil of the early rains   (:40
  Clouds that rain on the summer fruit
    Dew that falls on the grapes!
Seven years may Baal afflict thee
  Eight, the Rider of Clouds!
Let there be no dew
  Let there be no rain
    Let there be no surging of the Two Deeps   (:45
      Let there be no goodness of Baal's voice!"
As she tears the garb of Danel, Man of Rp',
  The garment of the Hero, Ma[n] of Hr[nmy]
Aloud to his daughter [he shouts]:
"Hear Pughat!   (:50
  Who shoulders wat[er]
    Pours dew on the barley
      Kno[ws] the course of the stars! [90]
Saddle an ass
  Hitch a donkey!
Place my trappings of silver
  My saddlery of gold!"
There hear[kens] Pughat   (:55
  Who shoulders water
    Pours dew [on the barl]ey
      Knows the course of the stars.
Weeping she saddles an ass
  Weeping she hitches a donkey

---

[90] These are the virtues of a model daughter: she looks after the water and food supplies, and is skilled at divining.

Weeping she lifts her father
　She sets him on the back of an ass
　　On the beautiful back of the donkey.   (:60
− − Danel turns his − − − −
　He sees the stalk in the − − − −
　　He sees the stalk in the patch.
He [embrac]es and kisses the stalk.
"Would I were a stalk springing up from the − − − !   (:65
　The stalk would spring from the patch of − − − −
May the hand of Aqhat the Hero gather thee
　May it set thee in the midst of the granary."
Ydnh [91] turns his food
　He sees the ear in the food
　　The ear springs forth from the dryness   (:70
He embr[aces] and kisses the ear:
"Would I were the e[ar]!
Let the ear spring from the food
　Let − − − spring forth!
May the hand of Aqhat the Her[o] gather thee
　Let it put thee in the midst of the granary."
The word had not yet gone out of his mouth   (:75
　From his lips, [his utterance]
When on lifting her eyes
　She sees
There is no [   ]
[   ] going − − − [   ] from my pot go[es out]
[   ] goes out and does not go out
Strike(s) [twice on the h]ead
　Thrice over the ea[r].
[　t]ies the locks of his head [   ]   (:80
　Over the lock [   ]
　　[   ] curls.[92]
And [his] wee[ping] is poured out like quarter-shekels [   ]
　Their face − − − − − − − −[   ]
　　Their face [   ]

[91] An alternative name for Danel, appearing only here.
[92] The locks and curls are typical of the early heroes; *cf.* the long-haired
Achaeans of Homer, Samson's locks, and especially the Minoan fashon of long
locks for men.

my – – –   – – – [   ]   (:85
I bring you news, Dan[el   ]
head [   ]
[Like a win]d, my [soul]
   Like a gust, my spirit.
There arrive [   ]
They lift [their] voice
   [And shout]:
"Hear, O Danel, Man (of Rpʾ)!   (:90
Aqhat the Hero is dead.
The Virgin Anath [has caused his soul to go out] like [wind]
   Like a gust, his spirit."
[On it the feet] jump
He [breaks] the back   (:95
[His vertebrae] are agitated.
[He lifts his voice]
   And shou[ts]:
"[   ] smiter [   ]
(*six lines broken*)
On lifting [his eyes]   (:105
   [Yea he sees]
[   ] enter [   ]
[He lifts his voice]
   And shouts:
"May Baal break [the wings of the eagles]
   May Baal bre[ak their pinions]
     That they may fall under my feet!
I'll spli[t their inwards and] look   (:110
If there is fat
   If there is bone
I shall weep
   And bury him
I'll put (him) in the grave of the gods of the earth."
The word had not yet gone from his mouth
   From his lips, [his] utterance
When Baal broke the wings of the eagles
   Baal broke their pinions   (:115
     So that they fell under his feet.
He splits their inwards and [looks]

There is no fat
   There is no bone.
He lifts his voice
   And shouts:
"May (Baal) repair the wings of the eagles
   May Baal repair their pinions!
Eagles!
Flee!   (:120
   And fly!
On lifting his eyes
   Yea he sees
He spies Hrgb
   Father of the eagles.
He lifts his voice
   And shouts:
"May Baal break the wings of Hrgb
   May Baal break [his] pinions
      So that he may fall under my feet!
I'll split [his] inwar[ds] and look   (:125
If there is fat
   If there is [bone]
I shall weep
   And bury him
I'll put (him) in the grave of the g[ods of the earth]."
[The word had not yet gone from his mouth]
   [From] his [lip]s, his utterance
When Baal broke the wings of Hrgb
   Baal broke his pinions
      So that he fell under his feet.   (:130
He splits his inwards and looks
There is no fat
   There is no bone.
He lifts [his] voice
   And shouts:
"May Baal repair the wings of Hrgb
   May Baal repair his pinions!
Hrgb!
Mayest thou flee
   [And] fly!"

On lifting his eyes
   Yea he sees   (:135
He spies Ṣml
   Mother of the eagles.
He lifts his voice
   And shouts:
"May Baal break the wings of Ṣml
   May Baal break her pinions
      That she may fall under my feet!
I'll split her inwards and look
If there is fat
   If there is bone   (:140
I'll weep
   And bury him
I'll put him in the grave of the gods of the earth."
The word had not yet gone from his mouth
   From his lips, his utterance
When [Ba]a[l broke] the wings of Ṣml
   Baal broke her pinions
      So that she fel[l under] his feet.
He splits her inwards and looks
There is fat   (:145
   There is bone
And he takes Aqhat therefrom
– – – – – –

He weeps and buries
   He buries him in a sepulcher
      In an *u*[*rn*]
And he lifts his voice
   And shouts:
"May Baal break the wings of the eagles
   May Baal break their pinions   (:150
If they fly over the grave of my son
   To disturb him in his sleep!"
(At) the well of w[ater] the king shouts:
"Woe unto thee, O well of water
   Along [side which] Aqhat the Hero was smitten
      Who abided longest in the house of El.
Now he has fled for eternity

Now and forevermore!"
He prepared Destiny (:155
    The staff of his hand.
He went to – – – – – – – – –
He lifts his voice
    And shouts:
"Woe unto thee, – – – – – – –
    Alongside which Aqhat the Hero was smitten!
May thy roots not flourish in the earth (:160
    My head is lowered through thy *perfidy*.
Now he has fled for eternity
    Now and forevermore!"
He prepared Destiny
    The staff of his hand.
He proceeds to the City of Mourners, Abilûma,
    The City of Prince Moon
He lifts his voice (:165
    And shouts:
"Woe unto thee, City of Mourners
    Near which Aqhat the Hero was smitten!
May Baal make thee one-eyed
From now and unto eternity
    Now and forevermore!"
He prepared Destiny
    The staff of his hand.
(And behold the house: one returns to the story) [93] (:side
Danel proceeds to his house (:170
    Danel reaches his palace
The weeping women enter his palace
    The wailing women, his court Pẓġm Ġr [94]
He weeps for Aqhat the Hero
    Sheds tears for the Child of Danel, Man of Rpʾ. (:175
From days to months
    From months to years
        Until the seventh year
He weeps for Aqhat the Hero

---

[93] The scribe apparently interrupted his copying, and made this note in the margin in order to remind himself where to begin upon returning.

[94] Perhaps the name of Danel's palace.

Sheds tears for the Child of Danel, Man of Rpʾ.
In seven years (:180
[Danel, Man] of Rpʾ, declares:
   The Hero, M[an of Hrnmy], proclaims:
[He] lifts his voice
   And shouts:
"De[part], weeping women, from my palace
   Wailing women, from my court Pzǵm Ǵr!"
And he ma[kes] a sacrifice (to) the gods (:185
   Offers up an offering into heaven
   The offering of Hrnmy, [that of the s]tars
(*three lines broken*)
Then declared Pughat (:190
   Who shoulders water:
"Make, O Father, a sacrifice to the gods
   Offer up an offering unto heaven
      The offering of Hrnmy, that of the stars!
Wilt thou not bless me that I may go blessed
   Protect me that I may go protected? (:195
I'll smite the smiter of my brother
   Yea destroy the destroyer of my [s]ibling!"
And [Dan]el, Man of Rpʾ, replies:
"By my soul let [Pughat] *live*
   Who shoulders water
      Pours dew on the barley (:200
         Knows the course of the stars
[   ] may she prosper!
Mayest thou smite the smiter [of thy brother]
   Destroy the destroyer of [thy] sibling!"
[   ] heart of the sea.
She wash[es]
   And rouges herself
      With a rouging from the husk of [   ]
Of a thousand acres, the *ẓuh*-fish in the sea [95] (:205
She dons a hero's garb
   She puts [a weapon in] its holder
      A sword she puts in [its] scabbard
And over (it) she wears a woman's garb.

[95] Can the *ẓuh*-fish be the murex, from which the rouge was made?

[From] the rising of the Luminary of the Gods, Sun, – – – – fields
  To the setti[ng] of the Luminary of the Gods, Sun.   (:210
Pughat reach[es] the tents.
Word is [br]ought to Yaṭ[pan]:
"Our mistress has come into thine abode
  [Pughat] has come hither."
And Yaṭpan, Soldier of the Lady, answers: (:215
"Receive her and give her to drink
  The wine of the cup in my hand
    The chalice in my right hand
Receive Pughat and give her to drink!"
She se[es the cup] in his hand
  The chalice in his right hand
And Yaṭpan, [Soldi]er of the Lady, declares:
"Of the wine *our* god Ilš drinks [   ]
  Who created the abode.   (:220
The hand that smote the Hero A[qha]t
  Will smite thousands of my lady's foes!
The lady of sorcery to the tents!"
Pu[ghat] like – – – – – her heart
  Like a serpent, h[issing   ]
Twice she drinks that mixture
  Drinks [that mi]xtur[e].

Texts 121–124 may have some connection with the Aqhat Cycle. Danel is in any case mentioned in text 121:I. These texts deal with the chariot-riding deities called Rapaʾûm who visit Danel. These texts also deal with Baal and Anath in a way that connects them with the pervasive theme of fertility.

[   ] my – – – –   (122:1
"Go to my house, [shades]
  [To] my [palace] I invite you, I call [you]."
[those who des]troy his place.
The shades [   ] his place
  Do not the deities proceed?
[   ] my – – – –   (:5
Thereupon – – – [   ]
you, my friends; now I go [   ]

thirty, I proceed to the house
[   ] my palace.
And El replies: [   ]
"Go to my house, shades
　[To my palace I invi]te, I call you."   (:10
[those who destr]oy his place
The shades [   ] his [place]
Do not the de[ities] proceed?
[   ]
[   ] on/to earth [   ]
(*rest broken*)
[   ] they/ye sacrifice   (121:I:1
[   ] deities
[   ] I shall die
[   ] and she enters − − −
[   ] on a day of summer   (:5
[   ] they eat
　[   ] they drink
[   ] god of the ᶜ*rgz*-plants
[   ] on − − −
[   ] sacrifice − − −   (:10
[   ]
eight in the midst of my palace.   (121:II:1
They go to his place, the de[ities] go
the grooms of horses harness [   ]
They mount on their chariots
　They co[me]
They go a day and a second   (:5
　After su[nrise] on the third day
The shades come to the threshing floors [   ] plantings.
And Danel, [Man of Rp'], replies
　The Hero, Man of Hrnmy, retorts:
"On the threshing floors, O gods, in the midst of [   ]
wherein they come, they will surely eat [   ]   (:10
apple(s), − − − −　− − −[   ]"
(*end broken*)
And [   ]   (:123:1
in my palace [   ]
"Go to my house, O sh[ades]

[To my palace I call], I invite you."

[   ] his place.   (:5

The s[hades   ]

  Do not the de[ities] proceed

    The soldiers of Baal

      [And the soldiers] of Anath?

"Go to [my] hou[se, O shades]

  [To my palace] I call, [I invite] you." [   ]

to my palace, [his] place, [shades]   (:10

his place, do not [the deities] pro[ceed]?

barefoot – – – –

Hear ye [   ]

day/sea, for – – [   ]

oil, half-shekel [   ]   (:15

he vows them, a day [   ]

over – – – – – – [   ]

the dais, the throne of [sovereignty]

I call the shades [   ]

in the midst of [my] pa[lace]   (:20

they go to his place [   ]

the chariot[eers   ]

they mount on [their] cha[riots]

their cities/asses [   ]

in [   ]

(*end broken*)

him, behold thy son, behold [   ]   (124:2

sons of the sons of thy place, behold [   ]

thy hand(s), little one, kiss thy lips, there

shoulder to shoulder, brothers *resurrected* of El   (:5

in running there – – – – the name of El, men

– – – – bless me, name of El, heroes there – – – – –

There are the shades of Baal

  Soldiers of Baal

    And soldiers of Anath.

There, (go) barefoot the forces of the Prince   (:10

  Of King ᶜllmy

As Anath goes to hunt

  She *takes off* in flight heavenward.

Slaughtered are great and small cattle

Felled are oxen and fatling rams
  Year-old bullocks
    Tiny lambs, kids.
Like silver for *merchants*   (:15
  Olive oil of gold for *merchants*
Like fields of fruit of the table
  The *daintiest* of *dainties* of kings.
Behold a day he pours wine of *ṭmk*
  Must, the wine of *srnm*
Wine, not of gleanings
  Wine, first-class.
O giants of the range of Lebanon   (:20
Wine dew El has plowed.
Lo a day and a second
  The shades eat
    They drink
A third, a fourth day
A fifth, a sixth day
  The shades eat
    They drink
In the dining hall
  In – – –
    In the heart of Lebanon   (:25
Lo on the seventh day
[   ] Aliyan Baal
(*rest broken*)

Several other mythological fragments have been published such as
texts 1001–1003 and 2001–2004, but none have yielded connected
sense yet. Other fragments have been unearthed but still await full
publication. One of them states: "She eats his flesh without a knife
and drinks his blood without a cup" (*UT*, p. 372, no. 467). M. C.
Astour has recognized in this a forerunner of wild Bacchic rites in
which living victims were torn apart and devoured. Fourteen mythological and liturgical texts found at Ugarit in the twenty-fourth
campaign (1961) will be published by Charles Virolleaud in

Ugaritica V, as Chapter III (pp. 545–595 of the page proofs kindly sent to me by the excavator, Claude Schaeffer, in November, 1965).

Much of Ugarit remains to be excavated, and more tablets will eventually be unearthed. Meanwhile, the known but difficult fragments will gradually fit into place and become more intelligible.

Chapter V

THE PROSE TEXTS
OF UGARIT

The excavations at Ugarit have produced a host of prose texts in Ugaritic and Akkadian ranging from royal letters to treatises on the care of horses. Most of the Akkadian texts deal with the royal circle and international affairs. In fact, the Akkadian texts published by Jean Nougayrol in *PRU* III and IV make Ugarit one of the best-known city-states of remote antiquity, with respect to both internal and external political life.

Although our detailed knowledge of Ugaritic administration and politics does not begin until the reign of Niqmad II (who ruled until about 1345 B.C.), we know that his father was King Ammistamru I, who reigned over Ugarit in the Amarna Age. The dynasty, however, went back centuries earlier. The dynastic seal,[1] used by the later kings of Ugarit, portrays a seated deity, with a cup in his hand, blessing a standing man, behind whom stands a goddess with flounced robe and raised hands. Such scenes with seated gods are typical of the Ur III period (*ca.* 2000 B.C.) but continued to be used during the Babylon I period, especially during the early part of it. This seal may well date from around the nineteenth century B.C. The inscription of the seal tells us that its original owner was "Yaqarum the son of Niqmad King of Ugarit." We refer to this Niqmad as Niqmad I. We know little about him except what may be inferred from this seal. Whether "King of Ugarit" refers to him, or only to his son Yaqarum, is not clear. But we do know that at least two kings of the dynasty were called "Niqmad" after him. It

[1] See the photographs in *PRU* III, plate XVI.

may be that Yaqarum was the first king of the dynasty, and that Niqmad was considered the ancestor of the line. Both names are Semitic, like all the subsequent royal names of the line, with the lone exception of "Arḫalba," which is Hurrian.

The dynasty endured from the nineteenth century B.C., when Yaqarum's seal was probably carved, until the beginning of the twelfth century, when the Ugaritic kingdom came to an end: a span of over six hundred years. Hitherto the longest known dynasty of a kingdom in Canaan has been the Judean House of Jesse, founded by his son David around 1000 B.C., and terminated in 586 B.C. during the reign of David's descendant Zedekiah, when Nebuchadnezzar destroyed Jerusalem and the city-state of which it was the capital.

The documented history of Ugarit fits into known world history from about 1380 B.C., in the Amarna Age, until the invasion of the Sea People around 1195.[2]

Down into the Amarna Age, Ugarit was under heavy Egyptian influence. Amarna Letter 45 mentions Ammistamru I as loyal to Egypt. This influence is suggested also by Egyptian objects found at Ugarit, including a scarab of Amenophis III (about 1413–1377 B.C.).

Niqmad II came to the throne during the reign of Amenophis IV (known as "Ikhnaton") (about 1377–1358 B.C.) and reigned over Ugarit until about 1345. Amarna Letter 49 was written by Niqmad II to keep up contact with Ikhnaton. A fire devastated much of Ugarit in Niqmad's reign, but the palace was rebuilt, and the royal records that have been excavated are those which were maintained from that time to the end of the dynasty.

Fragments of a vase found at Ugarit bear inscriptions of the names of Ikhnaton and Nefertiti, along with "Niqmad, the Great One of the land of Ugarit" in Egyptian, reflecting the close ties between Ugarit and Egypt.

It was during the reign of Niqmad II that the Hittites, under King Shuppiluliuma I (*ca.* 1380–1346 B.C.), defeated Tushratta, king of

---

[2] The main source of the following sketch is the copies of texts in *PRU* IV, where the reader can find the tablets arranged according to the successive reigns and then conveniently broken down into dossiers. Liverani's *Storia di Ugarit* is also useful.

Mitanni, and emerged as the leading power in Asia. Shuppiluliuma widened his sphere of influence into Syria, engulfing the little kingdom of Ugarit. Niqmad was persuaded to aid the Hittites in their wars against the Syrian states, and Shuppiluliuma rewarded his loyalty by enlarging his boundaries. Ugaritic text 118 is the list of tribute that Niqmad II paid to Shuppiluliuma and his courtiers. The Hittites did not cut off Ugarit from any part of the world, not even Egypt. It was in everyone's interest to maintain trade and prosperity, so that Ugarit, though militarily a vassal state within the Hittite system, was permitted to run its own internal affairs and to carry on its trade with the rest of the world. It was during the reign of Niqmad II that scribes such as Elimelech copied the main literary texts that have been discovered

Niqmad II was succeeded by his son Arḫalba (*ca.* 1345–1336 B.C.), who at first continued to serve as a vassal of the Hittites under Mursil II (*ca.* 1345–1315). The city of Carchemish now began to represent the Hittite Empire in many regional affairs concerning its Syrian vassals, including Ugarit. Arḫalba's reign began just after the death of Shuppiluliuma, which touched off a spate of rebellions against the Hittites in Syria. We do not know whether Arḫalba actually helped the rebels. What we do know is that when Mursil II had the situation well in hand, he put Arḫalba's brother Niqmepa, another son of Niqmad II, on the throne of Ugarit. At the same time there is reason to believe that Arḫalba had planned to have the line continued through his brother. Arḫalba was childless, and so he willed that his wife, Kubaba, should, after his death, be wed to his brother and that no other man should take her for himself. In this arrangement, known as levirate marriage, a living brother continues the marriage by taking the place of his deceased brother, so that progeny may carry on the family line in direct succession.

Niqmepa (*ca.* 1336–1265 B.C.) had a long and prosperous reign. To be sure, Ugarit was stripped of its jurisdiction over its southern neighbors, Siyannu and Ushnatu, but a commensurate reduction of Ugarit's tribute to the Hittites lightened the blow. Moreover, Mursil confirmed Niqmepa in his possession of the Mukish cities along the northern frontier of Ugarit that had been awarded to Niqmad by

Shuppiluliuma as a reward for faithful vassalage on the battlefield.

Niqmepa ended his long reign as a vassal of Hattusil III (*ca.* 1283–1250 B.C.). Merchants sponsored by Hattusil were causing problems in Ugarit. The Hittite king therefore regulated the merchants' activity there. On the one hand, their Ugaritic debtors were forced to pay what they owed under penalty of being seized, together with their wives and children, by the merchants. On the other hand, the merchants were not allowed to settle in Ugarit; they were forbidden to reside there in the winter season or to buy real estate there. It is interesting to note that these merchants came from Ur(a), a city bearing the same name as the city where Abraham was born.

Hattusil respected the Ugaritic king's jurisdiction over slaves and subjects to the point of promising to extradite them in case they fled to the Hapiru terrain of the Hittite king.

The great international event in Niqmepa's reign was the Battle of Kadesh, when Ramses II (*ca.* 1301–1234 B.C.) came to grips with Muwattal (brother and a predecessor of Hattusil) around the year 1296. The very fact that the battle did not result in a decisive victory for either side helped serve a constructive purpose. The two nations came to terms with each other, and around 1267 B.C. Ramses not only married Hattusil's daughter but made her his queen. The Battle of Kadesh resulted in enduring peace between the two empires, and incidentally confirmed Ugarit's position within the Hittite sphere, since the Kadesh line was far south of Ugarit.

Niqmepa was succeeded around 1265 B.C. by his son Ammistamru II, who must have had a long reign, judging from the large number of his edicts and of the political documents pertaining to him. Ammistamru was a younger son of the aged Niqmepa. Ugarit was profiting from the long peace between the Egyptians and Hittites, and its traders were enriching the Ugaritic treasury. We find Ammistamru spending 50 minas of gold to buy his way out of helping the Hittites militarily against Assyria, and paying 1,400 shekels of gold to avenge himself on a wife who has offended him. In his material prosperity and his trouble with women he is somewhat reminiscent of Solomon. Niqmepa's widow, Queen Aḫât-milku, was,

like Bathsheba, an influential personage and may have ruled for a
while as regent or coregent. And like Solomon, Ammistamru had to
contend with brothers who aspired to his throne.

Initeshub, the great-grandson of Shuppiluliuma, was now king of
Carchemish and was active in regulating the affairs of Ugarit. Thus
when two sons of Queen Aḫât-milku wronged Ammistamru and
their mother [3] (apparently challenging their authority), Initeshub
decreed that the two offenders should take their inheritance and go
into exile on the island of Cyprus (Alashiya).

International marriages and divorces among the Hittite vassals
were diplomatic matters subject to regulation by the Hittite king
and his agents. Tudhaliya IV (*ca.* 1250–1220 B.C.) thus laid down
the provisions for Ammistamru's divorce from the daughter of
Benteshina, king of Amurru. The material terms of the divorce
settlement resemble those between any divorced man and wife.
More interesting are the clauses pertaining to the divorcee's son,
who was heir to the throne, in that they forbid him to rejoin his
mother during the lifetime of his father, on pain of losing the right
of succession.

Ammistamru had more wife trouble, this time with "the Daughter
of the Great Lady," another Amurru princess. She committed some
"great sin" against him, with the result that he took steps against
her and she fled to her native land, where Shaushgamuwa had
succeeded Benteshina to the throne. King Shaushgamuwa sided with
Ammistamru but refused to extradite her to Ugarit. However, Ammistamru finally got his way by offering 1,400 shekels of gold to the
king of Amurru, who handed over his kinswoman to be killed, now
that the price was right.

Amurru was famed for its people's capacity for intrigue. Twice
Ammistamru committed the mistake of marrying Amurru princesses.
We do not specifically know what they did to offend him. Their
intrigues were perhaps of a political nature, calculated to undermine
the position of their husband.

Ammistamru was succeeded by his son Ibiranu. The latter was
remiss in reporting, and sending gifts, to his Hittite lord and was

[3] Whether she was Ammistamru's mother or stepmother is not yet clear.

reprimanded for it. Also the king of Carchemish had to remind him to contribute his stint of soldiers and chariots.

The long dynasty of Niqmad was coming to its end. Ibiranu was succeeded by his son Niqmad III, whose reign was short. The last king of Ugarit was Ammurapi (the name corresponds to that borne of old by the great Hammurapi of Babylon), about whom our knowledge is scant.

Around 1195 b.c., early in the reign of Ramses III (*ca.* 1197–1165), a wave of Sea People brought to an end the Hittite Empire. With it Ugarit disappeared from the course of history.

The administrative documents of the Ugaritic court cannot be described here in detail.[4] Many of them deal with land grants. In general it may be said that the king of Ugarit could dispose of real estate as he wished. He could take land from his subjects and transfer it to other subjects more to his liking. With the receipt of real estate there usually went the feudal obligation to serve the king economically or in battle. The king, however, could exempt his favorites from this obligation. The picture we get is that the king could give and take back at will. The subjects on the losing end could resent his action but do nothing about it legally. We are reminded of how Achilles resented, but did not contest the legality of, Agamemnon's taking back the prize that he had awarded him (*Iliad* 1:299). When Job says (1:21) "Yahweh has given and Yahweh has taken away, blessed be the name of Yahweh," he is attributing to God the conventional right of kings: to take back what they have given. As arbitrary and unjust as this principle seems, it served the purpose of stabilizing the nation, for the power of the king was not dissipated among his barons. As long as the king could take back what he had given to them, central authority would not give way to feudal decentralization.

The administrative documents give us a good picture of the society and its relation to, and regulation by, the government. Aside from the peasants and herdsmen, the people tended to be grouped

---

[4] The abundant material in Akkadian is readily available in *PRU* III. For a sketch of the administrative texts in Ugaritic, see C. H. Gordon, *Ugaritic Literature,* pp. 122–127.

according to hereditary guilds. Builders, smiths, potters, and count-less types of craftsmen all had their guilds. The same held for pro-fessions, including the military and the priesthood. The ruling class infiltrated the military and religious guilds, thus cementing its hold on the nation.

Last, but not least, the proper names in the prose texts are the key to the ethnography of Ugarit, and incidentally confirm its links with the Aegean and with Israel. *PRU* V confronts us with personal names such as *Mn*, "Mino-s," and *Ddl*, "Daedal-us," recalling the names of the two leading figures in Minoan civilization. The Ugaritic counterparts to Hebrew names include *Yšril*, "Israel"; *Abrm*, "Ab(i)ram"; *Mṯ*, "Moses," and *Išbᶜl*, "Eshbaal," to mention only a few of the numerous onomastic tie-ins with early Hebrew literature.

No future history of early Greece or Israel (to say nothing of the ancient Near East as a whole) can afford to neglect the rich and important documentation of Ugarit.

Chapter VI

CONCLUSIONS

Ugaritic literature is shedding a flood of new light on the origins of Western culture. The *Epic of Kret*, with its Helen-of-Troy motif, anticipates the greatest epic of the West—Homer's *Iliad*. At the same time it shows quite plainly what had not been seen before: that the same motif forms a major strand in the Patriarchal Narratives of Genesis wherein kings wrest the beautiful Sarah from Abraham, the progenitor of kings. This Ugaritic parallel is particularly important because it is simultaneously associated with Greek and Hebrew literatures. Ugarit is the best-known link between the two. No serious study of Western civilization can afford to disregard this fully established, but as yet insufficiently recognized, fact.

Old Testament scholars are familiar with the phenomenon of Hebraic opposition to the Canaanite milieu. However, the application of this principle is still in its infancy. The Ten Commandments, for instance, cover precepts that are more or less universally accepted, along with others that are anything but universal. The commandments not to steal or to commit adultery can be paralleled in almost any society, and are enforceable by law. But the commandment not even to covet the other fellow's property or wife is anything but universal and cannot be enforced by law. Indeed, the materialistic Western ideal today is precisely to covet one's neighbor's possessions, not as a prelude to stealing them, but as an incentive to exert oneself toward winning a better material status. Not only the slightly reprehensible "keeping up with the Joneses," but also the highly respectable goal of "raising one's standard of living," goes hand in hand with "coveting" one's neighbor's earthly goods. In Canaan "coveting" was not opprobrious. To the contrary, the Ugaritic texts tell us that Baal was a coveting god, using the same

151

word (*ḥmd*) as in the Ten Commandments. Accordingly, the emphasis on not coveting in Israel was prompted in opposition to the honored values of pagan Canaan, now on record for the first time in the Ugaritic poems.

Consider also a classical problem solved by primary sources in the foregoing pages. Ugarit was a West Semitic community with a Hurrian minority that exerted considerable influence in religious matters. Among the gods worshiped at Ugarit were the Hurrian deities Kumarbi and the storm god Teshub, who correspond to Cronus and Zeus respectively. Hesiod tells of how Zeus displaced his father Cronus, in the *Theogony*, 453–505. The details (including the crude plan of Cronus to swallow all his children as they came forth from the womb so that none might succeed him as king, and how he was foiled by his son Zeus) are so close to the Kumarbi Myth that classical scholars universally recognize the dependence of the Greek theogony on the Hurrian. Hesiod (lines 477 and 480) locates the story on Crete. The Minoan texts from Hagia Triada, Crete, contain two unmistakable Hurrian names, so that now we have the channel of transmission. It now appears that the Hurrian minority on Minoan Crete introduced the myth to the Aegean.

Multiply these samples by a thousand, and you will have a rough idea of what is in store for the history of Greek and Hebrew origins and consequently of our own Western culture, secular and religious.

Ugaritic literature has bridged the gap between Homer and the Bible. Thanks to the Minoan texts we know that from about 1800 to about 1400 B.C., Greece was dominated by Northwest Semites ("Phoenicians"), who linked it linguistically and culturally with the whole Semitic Levant. The culture of the East Mediterranean had already absorbed the best that antiquity had to offer, embracing the Sumero-Akkadian heritage in the east and the Egyptian legacy in the west.

Neither Greece nor Israel had to go abroad to borrow the rich contributions of Babylonia, the Nile Valley and other civilized areas of the Near East. The Sumero-Akkadian, Egyptian, Canaanite, and other heritages were built into the international culture entrenched on Greek and Palestinian soil before the Greeks and Hebrews of the Heroic Age in the second millennium appeared as historic entities. This means that the earliest Greek and earliest Hebrew literatures can be used to elucidate each other in the same way that Hittite records have been used to clarify Mycenaean Greek history, or that Egyptian and cuneiform texts have been brought to bear on early biblical problems. There is no longer any barrier between the early cultures of Europe and those of the Near East. Each is part of the same Mediterranean synthesis, whose written history begins in the Early Bronze Age (third millennium B.C.) and whose prehistory is attested by artifacts in the fourth millennium B.C.

These perspectives are in the course of opening a new era in the study of the origins and character of our civilization. The Ugaritic tablets give us a glimpse into the thought and literature of the East Mediterranean culture underlying our own. The Minoan texts demonstrate that essentially the same language and civilization permeated "Greece," before Greece was Greek.

INDEX

Aaron, 23n.
Abilûma, 129n.
Abimelech, 28
Ab(i)ram, 150
Abraham, 25, 27, 147, 151
Abrm, 150
Achaeans, 133n.
Achilles, 149
acrophony, 33
Adam, 102n.
Addu. *See* Hadd
administrative records, Ugaritic, 15, 149–150
Ādôn, 19
"Adonis," 19
adoption, 96n.
ᵓA-du, 36
Adventures in the Nearest East (Gordon), 36
Aegean, 11, 13, 15, 16, 20, 28, 131n., 150, 152. *See also* Greece; Mycenaean Greeks
"Aegean Writing and Linear A" (Pope), 32n.
Aegyptus, 32
Agamemnon, 149
ᵓa-ga-nu, 36, 38n.
ᵓA-ga-ru, 36
Ah-, 23n.
Aḫât-milku, 147–148
ahd(m), 44n.
"Ahijah," 31
Ahira, 31
ᵓᵃḫî-raᵉ, 31
"Ahmose," 23n.
Aigyptos, 58n.
Akkadian (language), 15, 16, 19, 20, 30n., 35, 144
Alalakh, 14, 37
Alashiya. *See* Cyprus
Alcmene, 97n.
Alexander, Conquest by, 14n.
alphabet, 15, 15n., 35
altars, mountain, 30
Amarna Age, 17, 17n., 144, 145

Amarna Letter, 145
Amarna Order, 12, 13, 17
Amenophis III, 17n., 145
Amenophis IV. *See* Ikhnaton
Ammistamru I, 144, 145
Ammistamru II, 147–148
Ammurapi, 149
Amon-Re, 58n.
Amphitryon, 97n.
Amurru, 66n., 148
a-na-i-ta, 38n.
a-na-ta, 38n.
Anath, 19, 21, 26, 41, 49n., 50n., 51n., 52n., 56n., 94n. *See also* Baal and Anath Cycle
Anath text translated, 48–62
Anatolia, 13, 14, 16, 17, 29. *See also* Hittites
annunciation formula, 24
anthropomorphism, 42n.
Antiquities (Josephus), 26n.
antonyms, 50n., 103n.
Apodulu, 32
Apodulu bowl, 35
APPLE sign, 32, 33
Aqhat, 25–26, 121n., 131n.
Aqhat, Epic of, 25–27, 33, 33n.
    translated, 120–139
Arabic (language), 20, 35, 103n.
Aramaic (language), 20, 35, 125n.
a-ra-na-re, 31
architecture, Minoan, 125n. *See also* palaces, Minoan
    spread of particular features, 18
Arḫalba, 145, 146
art, Minoan, 14
artifacts, reliance upon, 13
arts and crafts, god of, 58n. *See also* Kothar-and-Ḫasis
Arwad, 49n.
Asherah, 19, 21, 31, 36, 58n., 107n., 113n.
Ashkenazic Jews, 30n.
Asia, 12, 14, 17, 18, 146
Assyria, 147

155